T0114084

Cambridge Elements ≡

Elements in Publishing and Book Culture
edited by
Samantha Rayner
University College London
Leah Tether
University of Bristol

READING SPACES IN SOUTH AFRICA, 1850–1920S

Archie L. Dick

University of Pretoria

CAMBRIDGE
UNIVERSITY PRESS

CAMBRIDGE
UNIVERSITY PRESS

University Printing House, Cambridge CB2 8BS, United Kingdom

One Liberty Plaza, 20th Floor, New York, NY 10006, USA

477 Williamstown Road, Port Melbourne, VIC 3207, Australia

314–321, 3rd Floor, Plot 3, Splendor Forum, Jasola District Centre,
New Delhi – 110025, India

79 Anson Road, #06–04/06, Singapore 079906

Cambridge University Press is part of the University of Cambridge.

It furthers the University's mission by disseminating knowledge in the pursuit of
education, learning, and research at the highest international levels of excellence.

www.cambridge.org
Information on this title: www.cambridge.org/9781108814706
DOI: 10.1017/9781108887076

© Archie L. Dick 2020

This publication is in copyright. Subject to statutory exception
and to the provisions of relevant collective licensing agreements,
no reproduction of any part may take place without the written
permission of Cambridge University Press.

First published 2020

A catalogue record for this publication is available from the British Library.

ISBN 978-1-108-81470-6 Paperback
ISSN 2514-8524 (online)
ISSN 2514-8516 (print)

Cambridge University Press has no responsibility for the persistence or accuracy of
URLs for external or third-party internet websites referred to in this publication
and does not guarantee that any content on such websites is, or will remain,
accurate or appropriate.

Reading Spaces in South Africa, 1850–1920s

Elements in Publishing and Book Culture

DOI: 10.1017/9781108887076
First published online: November 2020

Archie L. Dick
University of Pretoria
Author for correspondence: Archie L. Dick, archie.dick@up.ac.za

ABSTRACT: Voluntary societies and government initiatives stimulated the growth of reading communities in South Africa in the second half of the nineteenth century. A system of parliamentary grants to establish public libraries in country towns and villages nurtured a lively reading culture. A condition was that the library should be open free of charge to the general public. This became one more reading space, and others included book societies, reading societies, literary societies, debating societies, mechanics institutes, and mutual improvement societies. This Element explains how reading communities used these spaces to promote cultural and literary development in a unique ethos of improvement, and to raise political awareness in South Africa's colonial transition to a Union government and racial segregation.

KEYWORDS: reading, voluntary societies, reading spaces, improvement, reading communities

© Archie L. Dick 2020

ISBNs: 9781108814706 (PB), 9781108887076 (OC)
ISSNs: 2514-8524 (online), 2514-8516 (print)

For Cali, Kelis, and Lacie

Contents

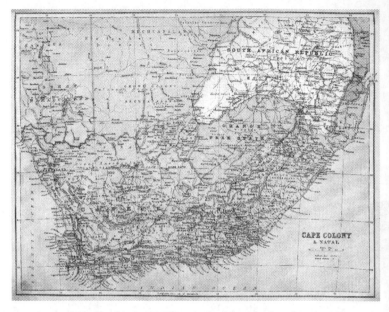

Map 1 South(ern) Africa, 1897, just before the South African War. Getty
Images / duncan1890

Basic South Africa Historical Timeline*

ca. 8000 BC: San hunter-gatherers inhabit the south western regions of southern Africa.

From AD 200: The semi-nomadic Khoikhoi begin farming the land.

From 1100: Other African peoples migrate into the southern African region from the north.

1488: Portuguese navigator, Bartolomeu Dias, lands at Mossel Bay.

1497: Vasco da Gama discovers a sea route to India via the Cape.

1652: Jan van Riebeeck sets up a supply station for the Dutch East India Company.

1667: Malay political exiles arrive at the Cape.

1688–1700: Huguenot refugees settle in the Cape.

1779: First of nine frontier wars.

1795: The British annex the Cape.

1803: The Cape Colony reverts to Dutch rule.

1806: Britain reoccupies the Cape.

1814: The Cape is formally ceded to Britain by the Dutch government.

1818: Shaka becomes king of the Zulus.

1820: British settlers arrive in the Eastern Cape.

1820–28: Shaka extends his territory, leaving large areas devastated and depopulated in his wake.

1834: Slavery is abolished.

1836–54: The Great Trek. Over 16,000 Voortrekkers travel northwards from the Cape in order to escape British domination.

1838: Voortrekkers under Andries Pretorius defeat the Zulus under Dingane at Blood River in Natal.

1845: Natal becomes a British colony.

1848: British sovereignty is proclaimed between the Vaal and the Orange rivers.

* Adapted from South Africa historical timeline. www.insightguides.com/destinations/africa-middle-east/south-africa. Accessed 20 May 2020.

1852: Boers found the Zuid-Afrikaansche Republiek.

1854: The Boer Independent Republic of the Orange Free State founded.

1867: Diamonds discovered at Kimberley.

1877: Britain annexes the South African Republic.

1879: The British defeat the Zulus at Ulundi.

1880–1: The Transvaal declares itself a republic. First Anglo-Boer War.

1883: Boer leader Paul Kruger becomes the first president of the Transvaal.

1886: Gold mining begins in the Transvaal and the mining town of Johannesburg is founded.

1899–1902: The South African War, or second Anglo-Boer War.

1910: The Union of South Africa is proclaimed.

1912: The South African Native National Congress is formed, known after 1923 as the African National Congress (ANC).

1913: The Native Land Act is passed, limiting land ownership for Blacks.

1925: Afrikaans replaces Dutch as the official 'second language' after English.

1948: National Party wins general election. Acts enforcing apartheid follow.

Introduction

During the War of Ngaryecibi, a copy of *The Pilgrim's Progress* and notes in isiXhosa and English were found on a fatally wounded 'native' in Piri forest, near King Williams Town.[1] The story was reported in the *Fort Beaufort Advocate* on 19 April 1878, and carried by other 'frontier' newspapers.[2] What struck the colonial volunteers who retrieved the body for burial was not just that this 'native' had been reading John Bunyan's classic, but that he was dressed in 'a full suit of black broadcloth' and had 'a first-class field glass slung over his shoulder'. Paul Nkupiso's name was inscribed on the flyleaf of this First-Prize book for English Reading, awarded by the Lovedale Missionary Institution. But its reader on the battlefield was in fact Dukwana,[3] a lay preacher and church elder at the Chumie (Tyumie) mission station, near Lovedale in the Eastern Cape (Odendaal, 2012, p. 42). He had trained as a printer, and at the Lovedale Press had helped to publish four issues of the English–isiXhosa newspaper *Ikwezi* (*Morning Star*, August 1844–December 1845), as well as school and hymn books.

In a lecture to members of a mutual improvement society in Port Elizabeth later that year, Reverend Robert Johnston recalled that Dukwana maintained that he was not fighting civilisation or Christianity. He was instead fighting the English 'who have robbed us of our country, and are destroying us as people' (Hodgson, 1986, p. 204). In these dramatic events, we find references to reading, a reading community, printing, publishing, the circulation of books, voluntary societies, and ideas about self-improvement and 'becoming literary' in rural South Africa in the second half of the nineteenth century. For Dukwana, the challenge of

---

[1] Hodgson (1986), p. 205. This war from 1877–8 was the last of nine Frontier 'wars of dispossession' fought over a period of 101 years.

[2] For example, *Kaffrarian Watchman*, 17 June 1878, and *Queenstown Free Press*, 19 July 1878.

[3] Dukwana was the son of Ntsikana who was regarded by the Xhosa in the Eastern Cape as a prophet and the first Xhosa Christian. Hodgson, J. 'Dukwana' in *Religion Past and Present*. http://dx.doi.org/10.1163/1877-5888_rpp_SIM_03946. Accessed 21 December 2019.

being a 'committed Christian and also an African patriot' meant that like his belief and practice, his reading should be 'relevant to his immediate social and political context' (Hodgson, 1986, p. 205). Saul Dubow (2006, p. 24) argues that, in the early years of the nineteenth century Cape Colony, 'the language of improvement and civilization served to legitimate the colonial enterprise in the eyes of the colonists themselves'. This was not just to gain approval in the metropole, but to help them to establish a corporate sense of identity.

By the 1870s, however, there were other languages of improvement, and different ideas about identity and 'becoming literary'. The first British missionaries were from the upper working classes in newly industrialising areas, and they believed in 'aggressive self-improvement'. Similarly, European-based Moravian missionaries brought craft production as well as basic education, literacy, and books, as did the French and German missions (Elbourne & Ross, 1997, p. 32). The lending library in Genadendal run by the Moravian mission since 1823, for example, carried works in German, Dutch, and English. It was praised by a Cape literary magazine to be 'the best country library in the colony'.[4] But what the early missionaries understood by improvement was challenged and changed by converts and native inhabitants in the second half of the nineteenth century. As Elbourne and Ross (1997, p. 50) explain: 'What the missionaries saw as liberation in matters spiritual was not accompanied by the promised temporal improvement. The implications of this failure had still to be worked out'.

Much of this would happen in a range of indigenised voluntary societies, whose reading programmes and literary outputs heralded a new dawn both culturally and politically. 'Native' or African, and Dutch-Afrikaans voluntary societies, founded in the 1870s and 1880s, shared some of the features of existing English-language societies and associations. But they also developed unique qualities, and some designed programmes that nurtured alternative ways to 'become literary' and more politically aware. Book, reading, literary, debating, and mutual improvement societies were effective improvement initiatives in small towns, and they included public reading in their programmes. Mechanics Institutes were less successful because of

[4] *The Cape of Good Hope Literary Gazette*, 2 April 1832, p. 273.

their condescending features, and their libraries 'frequently consisted of a hotch-potch of books contributed as gifts by well-meaning and philan-thropically-minded people'. The Cape Town Mechanics Institute library was described in 1858 as 'small, but select' (Immelman, 1956, pp. 18, 21).

And this Institute's decline was explained as a typical Anglo-American transplant that did not take local conditions sufficiently into account. But other voluntary societies adapted with greater care to meet more pressing demands. Laura Weiss (2017) studied the literary and mutual improvement societies of Glasgow in the long nineteenth century, and she identifies their manuscript magazines as evidence of a unique movement of improvement. Although those societies had connections with adult education and libraries, their special differences were 'the production of 'improving' manuscript magazines ... and oral and written "criticisms" that were products of a quest to become "literary"' (Weiss, 2017, p. 12). These features, she argues, reveal a 'religiously-infused ethos of improvement developed within Scottish dissenting culture' (Weiss, 2017, p. 12). The formation of clubs and societies, in which these magazines were created to record their group reading and writing practices, typified the movement in Glasgow.

Reverend Robert Johnston, the missionary who spoke about Dukwana at the Port Elizabeth Mutual Improvement Society, was connected with the United Presbyterian Church of Scotland that had taken charge of the Glasgow African Missionary Society in 1847 (Hodgson, 1986, p. 201). He would have been familiar with, and a participant in, this 'religiously-infused ethos of improvement' that Weiss elaborates. Dukwana knew Johnston, as well as Tiyo Soga, who had studied in Scotland and translated the first part of *The Pilgrim's Progress* into isiXhosa, which was published at Lovedale Press in 1867 (Davis, 2018). Dukwana was their adviser when the Glasgow African Missionary Society sent them to establish the Mgwali mission station, near Stutterheim in the Eastern Cape. Literary historian David Attwell describes Soga's translation and Dukwana's possible attraction to the 'materiality of the book as magical icon' as the first instance of 'transculturation of enlightenment'.[5] He relates this claim to what John

---

[5] Attwell, who refers to 'the unnamed Xhosa soldier', probably did not know that the reader who died in battle was in fact Dukwana.

and Jean Comaroff described as Africans recasting 'European forms in their own terms . . . in the country's long history of symbolic struggle' (Attwell, 2006, p. 30).

He then proceeds to argue that the missionary enterprise was hugely consequential in the fields of literacy and book production. Whereas mission literacy had defined the terms on which a Black South African literature was to emerge, there were opportunities too. And in this way, Soga's adoption of the mission ethos and discourse in the English language entailed 'a transculturation into African terms of the aims and instruments of colonialism's civilising mission' (Attwell, 2006, pp. 32–3). This 'transculturation of enlightenment' was the challenge for Soga and succeeding generations to achieve emancipation salvaged from 'economic and political instrumentalism, imperialism and racism, and pressed into the service of all humanity' (Attwell, 2006, p. 33). Whether or not Attwell is correct that the events involving Soga and Dukwana mark 'the moment . . . in which a black literary culture first develops in South Africa', and that this 'transculturated enlightenment' resurfaced in the early 1990s as 'the recovery of human rights', are uncertain.

What is important, and what this Element attempts to do, is to expand the focus on Soga as representing the production and creative literary outputs of writers to include Dukwana as representing the consumption and creative literacy practices of readers. As a printer and publisher, Dukwana was also involved in producing instructive material for reading communities. In other words, Dukwana the reader and printer is as important as Soga the writer and translator in South Africa's story of literacy and literary culture. And it was in the indigenised spaces of voluntary societies that readers would help to shape a unique ethos of improvement in the long nineteenth century. Dukwana would have been aware of the mutual improvement and other voluntary societies in Port Elizabeth, where, by the 1880s, several had been founded and led by Africans themselves (Odendaal, 1993). Past students of Lovedale, Healdtown, St. Mathews and other mission schools, who had been members of their literary and debating societies, tended to form literary and mutual improvement societies across the Eastern Cape, and elsewhere (Switzer, 1997, p. 62).

Shadrach Bobi who studied at Lovedale and qualified as a teacher, for example, started a literary society in 1877 at a boys' school in Morija, Lesotho.[6] Gwayi Tyamzashe explained a few years later that societies like these were started by 'natives themselves independently of any European assistance', and represented 'the necessity of striving to secure their interests'.[7] More recently, Ntongela Masilela (2010, p. 247) elaborated that this was a 'search for independence, and an effort to establish the means of self-empowerment'. He explains that although these societies affirmed Christianity, the English language and English cultural and literary knowledge, they viewed vernacular newspapers such as *Isigidimi Sama-Xosa* (*The Xhosa Messenger*), *Leselinyana* (*The Little Light*), and others as playing a transforming role. Importantly, the earliest pieces of writing by native speakers published in the isiXhosa mission newspaper, *Umshumayeli Wendaba* in 1838/9, came from four young learners. Their dialogues probed the benefits of reading, writing, and printing, and 'the way the book speaks' (Opland, 2004, pp. 33–5).

The ethos of improvement that emerged in these early literacy and literary activities can be described by what Christopher Saunders (2010, p. 14) explains as 'some kind of collaboration and cooperation' between 'settlers and indigenous people'. Or as Tyamzashe (1884) succinctly put it: 'to help yourself after you have been helped half way. It is with civilization as with Christianity'.[8] This ethos typified Dutch-Afrikaans debating societies too. Whereas some had aligned with the Dutch Reformed Church and drew on Western European models, others favoured a secular approach adapted to local conditions. The vernacular newspapers in which African mutual improvement societies published and commented on members' lectures and debates, and the Dutch-Afrikaans debating societies' manuscript journals carrying members' original literary contributions, represent

---

[6] Shadrach Bobi. www.ancestors.co.za/general-register-of-native-pupils-and-apprentices-lovedale-missionary-institution/. Accessed 21 December 2019.

[7] A Native Society at Kimberley, *The Christian Express*, 1 April 1884. http://pzacad.pitzer.edu/NAM/xhosaren/writers/tyamzash/tyamzashQ.htm. Accessed 13 December 2019.

[8] Ibid.

a unique ethos of improvement that arose in the second half of the nineteenth century. These voluntary societies were also spaces where common readers could confront elites and challenge political authority.

In South Africa's book history, there are several examples of sites and spaces where reading was repurposed (Dick, 2012). What should not, however, be overlooked is that, like the social libraries in the United States and proprietary libraries in England, subscription libraries in South Africa were also voluntary societies (Glynn, 2018; Harris, 1971, p. 45). They were, in fact, modelled on the pattern of British proprietary libraries (Immelman, 1970, p. 82). Their histories are connected with this ethos of improvement, and to the larger story of language and literary development, growing political awareness, and cultural recreation in South Africa's colonial transition to Union government. A number of subscription libraries started out as voluntary book societies or reading societies and amalgamation boosted their collections as well as membership numbers and types of readers. Small-town initiatives were tentative, characterised by bankruptcy and resuscitation, and the libraries were often rendered moribund. At one point, Grahamstown Public Library, for example, had to sell some of its books in order to save itself (Immelmann, 1970, p. 81).

Some sought relief through special grants until eventually the Cape colonial government in 1855 started a system of financial aid to subscription libraries in country towns and villages. A condition was that the general public should be admitted to the library free of charge on certain days of the week. In 1874, this concession to the public became 'whenever the library is open' in new legislation that made grants available 'to encourage the formation and proper management of public libraries in the smaller towns of the Colony'.[9] As a result, the number of subscription libraries across the Cape Colony swelled from 55 in 1874 to 157 in 1909,[10] with subscription fees and government grants as their principal sources of income. Although some

---

[9] *Memorandum of Regulations to Encourage Public Libraries in the Smaller Towns of the Colony*. Printed by Order of the House of Assembly, 28th May 1874.

[10] Immelman, 1970, p. 78; *Cape of Good Hope Blue Book, 1909*. Cape Town: Saul Solomon, p. 188. There were 173 by 1930 in the Cape Province (Immelman, 1970, pp. 45–6).

libraries had absorbed earlier book and reading societies, the mutual improvement and the literary and debating societies that sprang up included reading as an integral component of their programmes. They often used the reading space of the libraries as the venue for their meetings, and members drew on library resources to prepare debates, lectures, and public readings of essays and poems.

A study of reading communities and their reading spaces in these voluntary societies across South African towns reveals important insights into their number, range, and types. By throwing light on some of their writing spaces as well, this Element also explains the place of readers as writers in the literary and cultural history of South Africa's long nineteenth century. Many of the primary sources that provide the basis for arguments, descriptions, and statistics in the ensuing sections of this Element are housed in the country's national libraries, and archival depots. These were supplemented by records found in countryside public libraries and archives, as well as university special collections. They include government blue books, parliamentary and library annual reports, library catalogues, newspaper articles, yearbooks, private correspondence and journals, census records, diaries, and biographies. We can now better understand the unique ethos of improvement that these reading communities cultivated.

Section Summaries

Section 1 sketches the emergence of reading communities in voluntary societies, and their amalgamation with subscription libraries, in small towns and settlements. Some members used them to leverage careers and to connect with strategic social networks. As government-supported 'public libraries' in the second half of the nineteenth century, many collaborated with literary, debating, and mutual improvement societies. These voluntary societies provided members and residents with opportunities to become more literate and more literary.

Section 2 describes how reading communities in rural towns challenged and re-framed the 'English' rhetoric and ethos of improvement. Dissatisfaction and a growing political awareness produced alternative approaches to education, rights, and progress. Dutch-Afrikaner debating societies crafted new ways of political participation that affirmed language rights and cultural expression. And African mutual improvement societies sought alternative political strategies that adapted received literacy and literary practices.

Section 3 explains that Charles Dickens' works were not just found and read in public libraries. In other voluntary societies they were performed, quoted, copied, critiqued, gifted, preached, and screened. And across anti-apartheid organisations in the twentieth century some were repurposed for protest and revolution. His early humoristic works, and the later works in which social criticism featured more prominently, assured Dickens' reputation in South Africa.

In Section 4, Charlie Immelman's diaries reveal what fiction he read and shared with others, and what films he watched in small towns of the Cape. Local literary figures were among the book selectors for libraries, and they contributed to building 'improving' collections. As Immelman's diaries reveal, however, entertainment and distraction trumped serious literature whether available in public libraries or screened in cinemas. But when his tastes eventually turned to more literary themes, he could use these libraries profitably.

Section 5 explains how an obscure but important Islamic reading community connected with global printing networks. Distinctive reading, writing, and printing practices guided its participation in the transnational Islamic book trade, and shaped literary-cultural developments. By the early twentieth century, an emerging pan-Islamic and pan-African outlook characterised an ethos of improvement that would prepare this community to face the challenges of segregationist and apartheid South Africa.

1 Becoming Literate, Becoming Literary

Emulating mid-Victorian British culture, Emma Rutherfoord (Rutherfoord & Murray 1968, p. 19) read Harriet Beecher-Stowe's *Sunny Memories* to her Cape merchant-class family in the drawing room in the evenings of November 1852. Privately, her father had spent 'morning and night' completing *Uncle Tom's Cabin*. And although her brother Frederic considered some of Dickens' works 'too long and trifling', he was reading *Bleak House*. Joseph, the family servant, was also fond of reading and when a serious illness concerned Emma about his deteriorating health she gave him *The Contrast*, a book about preparing for death.[11] Emma's concern for 'appropriate' reading material persuaded her to read Dutch evangelical tracts to nearby farmers and their poverty-stricken workers. They, in turn, carried the tracts to countryside villages to read and distribute to neighbours until they were worn (Rutherfoord & Murray, 1968, p. 131). A Sailors Home, a Young Men's Mental Improvement Society, and a Mechanics Institute also benefited from the Rutherfoord family library's discarded books. These private and shared reading practices stretched into rural towns and settlements, and stimulated the growth of reading communities.

The *Cradock Despatch* ran briefly in 1850, and was followed soon by other newspapers in English and Dutch in that town, just over 800 km from Cape Town (Picton, 1969, pp. 60–1). Here, in the evenings of that year, Samuel and Lucy Gray gathered with their Yorkshire servant Edith to read novels. Lucy described Miss Grierson's *Pierre and His Family; or, A Story of the Waldenses* as nearly a Victorian bestseller in the style of Charlotte Mary Yonge's novels. Whether the Grays were members of the Cradock Reading Society is uncertain, but similar works of fiction filled the shelves of its Reading Room. A request for a portion of ground on which to erect it was approved as early as 1842.[12] It was a 'thatched building of white-washed brick on stone foundations' that preceded the construction of the Cradock Public Library by several years (Hattersley, 1951, p. 50).[13] By the 1870s, this library's collection had grown considerably, and Olive Schreiner was a keen borrower. She also used the libraries at Hanover and Kimberley, as well as Fraserburg when she visited her sisters or worked as a governess to children on nearby farms (Immelman, 1970, p. 77).

Almost 850 km west of Cradock, the public library at Clanwilliam also started as a reading society, and became a treasure house for the poet

---

[11] Some middle class women, like Caroline Molteno, taught family servants how to read (Duff, 2011, p. 499).

[12] Cape Archives, KAB 556/02/975.

[13] Although called public libraries in contemporary documents, these were strictly speaking subscription libraries that allowed a measure of access to the public.

C. Louis Leipoldt from the age of eight. Here he found and read the works of Scott, Eliot, and Austen as well as those of Byron, Browning, and Tennyson, donated to the library by an English settler. Leipoldt worked briefly at this library, which still bears his name today.[14] In similar fashion, the writer and poet, Francis Carey Slater, served on library committees and helped to select books for small country towns such as Dordrecht, Peddie, Barkly East, and Matatiele (Immelman, 1970, pp. 74–6). The middle-class reading practices and spaces in the Cape Colony's small towns were replicated in the Colony of Natal, proclaimed as a British colony in 1843. From the capital city of Pietermaritzburg, Marian Churchill wrote in 1858 to a friend that 'We employ our evenings in sewing and reading aloud in turn. *Tom Brown's Schooldays* . . . gave great satisfaction to our lady listeners' (Child, 1979, p. 119). Her brother Joseph was a member of the Natal Society Library, and in Durban a Reading Society, a Mechanics Institute library, and Penny Readings in public buildings offered additional venues for reading.

Mission Stations

But these were not the only reading spaces in which to become more literate and literary in mid-nineteenth-century South Africa. Beyond these towns were even humbler locales where Black South Africans and 'those of mixed descent' read and wrote in unexpected ways. By 1849, the literacy rate of 4, 678 residents on thirty-one mission stations across the Cape Colony had already reached 25.36 per cent, and their numeracy rate was 62.87 per cent (Fourie *et.al.*, 2013, p. 26). At Theopolis mission station in the Eastern Cape, a fourteen-year-old girl had read all the books in the mission library two or three times over. She was reading Rowland Hill's *Village Dialogues* just before her untimely death (Jones, 1850, p. 552). Just over 1,000 km north west of Theopolis, in 1842, Johann Frederick Hein, a 'mixed race' youth of just seventeen years old, had started his own school in the Ugrabib location in the Northern Cape's Richtersveld (Strassberger, 1969, pp. 70–1).

---

[14] See Leipoldt-Nortier Library, Canwilliam. www.clanwilliam.info/clanwilliam-member-163.php. Accessed 16 December 2019.

As a young man he read to adults, wrote letters to the Rhenish Mission Society, and eventually became an ordained priest.

In the Eastern Cape's Kat River settlement, residents could access school libraries, a Reading Society, and a circulating library where several newspapers were available (Read, 1852, p. 123). The Reading Society used the open veld as a reading space for communal reading and discussion of current events that often culminated in letters to newspaper editors. The settlement's Dutch Reformed Sunday Schools, of which there were already eleven in 1839, taught literacy and the Dutch language to adults. When the Cape Colony's first scientific census was taken in 1865, there were 15,252 'Blacks and those of mixed descent' who could read and write, with the women out-numbering the men.[15] That number for 'Blacks' would reach 455,398 (about 9.7 per cent of the colony's population) fifty-six years later, with the men in the majority.[16]

About 300 kilometres north of this settlement, several hundred people who were baptised at the Bensonvale Wesleyan mission station were taught to read and write. The mission library there was better stocked than those at older mission stations, and the writings of Tiyo Soga were read throughout the region. The mission subscribed to fifteen journals, and seven private individuals subscribed to periodicals of their own choice. There were twenty-five who could read English and many were multilingual in English, Dutch, isiXhosa, and Sesotho (Odendaal, 2012, p. 31). It was here that John Parkies, an interpreter and aspiring law agent, led protests and constantly wrote letters to Cape officials, who saw him as a troublemaker. In 1869, under his guidance, a petition by 125 residents was sent to the Cape parliament on behalf of 18,000 'British subjects' who lived in the Wittebergen Native reserve where this mission station was located.[17] They complained about being subjected to arbitrary rule in spite of being entitled to be ruled by British law. And it was just a few years later

---

[15] *Census of the Colony of the Cape of Good Hope*, 1865, p. 63.

[16] *Report on the Third Census 1921*, 1924.

[17] In this 'Native' reserve, by 1865, there were 92 men and 100 women who could read. There were 75 of the men, and 30 of the women who could both read and write, *Census of the Colony of the Cape of Good Hope, 1865*, p. 61.

that a Muslim voter, Jongie Siers, as a 'British subject' quoted lines from one of the foremost British poets to remind Alfred Ebden, a White English-speaking political candidate, of his duty. Siers' letter to the *Cape Times* invoked George Herbert's lines for Ebden to: 'find out men's wants and will, and meet them there' (Bickford-Smith, 1995, p. 454).

Just over 200 kilometres north of Bensonvale, a mission library at Thaba 'Nchu in the Eastern Free State had been active already in 1841. Young mission residents changed their books weekly and were quizzed on their contents by the resident missionary. Schoolbooks had been printed there since 1826 (Broadbent, 1865, p. 198). And mission libraries at Peelton, Somerset East, and Umvoti[18] that were destroyed during the wars of dispossession in 1846 and 1850–3 had been quickly replaced with £5 libraries.[19] These developments sustained the steady growth of literacy and a reading culture among Black South Africans in rural areas.[20] Some missionary institution libraries became public libraries, used by Black subscribers as well as many 'Europeans' unable to pay the subscription fees.[21] Having opened its doors in 1864, the library of the Lovedale Missionary Institution, for example, was one of the largest in the country. By 1868, it had become a public library and issued about 2,000 books annually (Peters, 1974, p. 15). By 1905, it had forty-five subscribers and an average number of fifty visitors per day. Another example is the Blythswood Training Institution, in the former Transkei, whose library was opened to the public in 1889, and where there were seventeen Black subscribers by 1905.[22]

Several types of reading spaces feature in the story of Zippora Leshoai, who was born in the Northern Cape town of Colesberg in 1885. Zippora's father, Masupa, who had been taken by the Voortrekkers and could read and write Hollands (Dutch), sent her to a 'Coloured' school in Kimberley where she had a Scottish teacher. She loved reading, and the first book she

---

[18] Towns in the Eastern Cape and an area in Kwa-Zulu Natal today.

[19] These were booklets or tracts to the value of five British pounds.

[20] 53rd Annual Report of the South African Tract and Book Society, 1852.

[21] *Replies to Circular, 1873–4, CO 4692*, Cape Archives.

[22] *Cape of Good Hope Blue Book. Reports of Public Libraries for 1905*, p. 331.

bought was John Bunyan's *The Pilgrim's Progress* because her mother had read it in Sesotho. Her mother, who was from the Quthing district in Lesotho, had been educated by French missionaries. Zippora then bought *Uncle Tom's Cabin*, which she had read as a pupil at Healdtown School, near Fort Beaufort. Tim Couzens (1984, pp. 74–6) describes these literary and literary practices as follows: Zippora 'came to read Bunyan in English because French missionaries had taught her mother to read it in Sesotho ... [who] told her the stories in Hollands (Dutch). A combination of a smattering of education, four languages and a tradition of storytelling!' He could have complicated it further by adding Zippora's book-buying habit.

This was a practice among educated Black readers, confirmed in a survey of 12,000 Black eighth-grade school learners across the country in the early twentieth century. A question about books found in the homes of their parents confirmed the popularity of *The Pilgrim's Progress* (certainly on Zippora's bookshelf), which was listed among a total of 220 titles headed by *Robinson Crusoe*, *King Solomon's Mines*, *Robin Hood*, and *Black Beauty* (Cook, 1939, p. 115). As with Zippora, these book-buying, and reading-related practices were nurtured in other Black and 'mixed descent' children in homes and schools. This had been happening already in the town of her birth, Colesberg, in the 1850s. Although there was a Dutch-medium London Missionary Society school mainly for 'children of Hottentots and Bushmen', a number of 'Coloured' children attended the government school (Ludlow, 2012). In this 'pedagogic space', the Scottish-based Chambers Educational Course was introduced to children. The First and Second Books of Reading typically introduced learners to image and text relating to the 'world of children while at the same time conveying a moral message' (Ludlow, 2012, p. 151). Controversially, the Third Book attempted to normalise a distinction between 'barbarous' and 'civilized' nations.

Voluntary Societies and Public Libraries

Reading and books featured too in the programmes of voluntary and mutual interest societies. The second half of the nineteenth century saw an emphasis on the idea of 'improvement' that included Enlightenment-influenced reading initiatives (Dick, 2018). In the towns and villages of the Cape Colony, the Colony of Natal, and the republics of the Transvaal (ZAR) and the Orange Free State,[23] there was a significant growth in the number of book societies, reading societies or reading associations, mechanics institutes, mutual improvement societies, literary societies, literary and debating societies, and play-reading societies.[24] Dependent mainly on membership fees and voluntary initiative, some lasted for only a few years or merged with the government-funded public libraries, or they were incorporated into cultural and entertainment organisations. Their programmes were advertised and reported regularly in local newspapers, which grew in number and quality in the 1850s.

Job losses in England after parliamentary expenditure on printing was curtailed had led to the migration of several journalists and printers to the Cape and Natal colonies. By 1858, larger towns like Cape Town, Grahamstown, and Port Elizabeth had at least three newspapers. Soon thereafter smaller towns had an English, Dutch, or bilingual newspaper that carried news about the activities of their voluntary societies. In the Colony of Natal, the Durban Mechanics Institute's first rule in 1853 stipulated that there should be a newsroom, a reading room and a library 'for the moral and intellectual improvement of [the institute's] members and others' (Plug, 1993, p. 99).[25] Subscriptions, revenue from public lectures, and a government grant boosted the Mechanics Institute library's growth, and it was eventually renamed as the Durban Public Library. With financial support from the Natal colonial government, the town of Verulam, almost 30 km from Durban, also merged its 'Public Library with its Mechanics Institute' in 1887. The Natal government supported 'Reading Rooms' too in Pinetown, Greytown, Ladysmith, and Newcastle at which several colonial and British newspapers were available (Plug, 1993).

---

[23] After it was annexed in 1900, it became the Orange River colony.

[24] Literary and scientific societies in South Africa at that time are not included in this Section.

[25] Mechanics Institutes in Cape Town and Port Elizabeth also had libraries to supplement their lectures and programmes.

The ethos of 'improvement' that inspired these initiatives adapted to local conditions and literary tastes.[26] Colonial newspapers in Natal, for example, made space for literary fare such as original verse and prose fiction, written and submitted by local readers (Christison, 2012, p. 126). The *De Natalier*, *Natal Witness*, and *Natal Mercury*'s special Christmas annuals or supplements presented opportunities for writers and entertainment for readers. Besides spaces for reading and writing, there were spaces too for debating in some voluntary societies. Their programmes and activities pushed and pulled the meanings of 'literacy', 'literary', and 'improvement' in different directions. As in colonial Australia, many voluntary societies in South Africa emphasised reading and literacy, and they complemented the role of public libraries (Mansfield, 2000, p. 15). The book and reading societies, in which these skills were nurtured, typically preceded the founding of public libraries. In the Cape Colony, they had been active since the 1830s in small towns like Worcester, Swellendam, Stellenbosch, Clanwilliam, Somerset East, and Grahamstown, where subscribers met in makeshift or purpose-built Reading Rooms.[27]

Alexander Jardine, the librarian at the South African Public Library in Cape Town, initially arranged the supply of books to these societies to promote reading and 'the wider dissemination of the English language ... for individual enjoyments, colonial prosperity and improvement'.[28] The value of books imported from the United Kingdom to the Cape Colony increased dramatically in the second half of the nineteenth century. The figures rose from £18,070 (78 per cent of the total imported) in 1858 to £47,218 in 1878. For the period 1880 to 1909, it was a whopping £3,010,968, and represented 90 per cent of all the imported books for the three decades preceding the unification of South Africa in 1910.[29] *Lees-Vruchten*, the

---

[26] For the connection between a culture of improvement and literary societies in nineteenth century Glasgow, see Weiss, 2017.

[27] Some were short-lived. The Grahamstown Reading Society voted itself out of existence in 1833. For a Reading Society in Cape Town, see Dick (2018).

[28] *The Cape of Good Hope Literary Gazette*, June 1830, vol. 1(1): 12.

[29] Calculated from the *Cape of Good Hope Blue Books*. Other countries variously include the United States, Holland, Germany, France, Australia, India, Natal

quarterly journal of a Dutch Reading Society, circulated in Paarl, Stellenbosch, and towns in the Swartland region. But its efforts to promote the reading of new Dutch literature and history failed because it did not match reading tastes at the Cape (Conradie, 1934, p. 257–8). In Stellenbosch, however, there was a 'Hollandse Leeskring' or Dutch Reading Circle – for men only – that existed until 1843, and, by 1847, there was a Reading Room in the town.

As in Victorian Britain, countryside book and reading societies at the Cape and Natal could be conduits to influential political and social networks (Bassett, 2017). Their committee members were often also on other important committees in small towns. When struggling book and reading societies applied for financial assistance through library grants from the Cape Colonial government, they, however, moderated their elitist character. The reason was a grant condition that the ensuing library should be open to all members of the community. Although only library subscribers could borrow materials, non-subscribers or members of the public were entitled to use the collections during the library's opening hours. The number of amalgamations of book and reading societies with public libraries grew as a result of these grants. This happened in 1857 at Murraysburg, a town with residents predominantly of mixed descent, and at Uitenhage in 1858, where the Reading Society was already established in 1825. In 1858 also, the Victoria West Reading Society had opened its reading room to the public free of charge, four years before it officially became a public library.

At Hanover, in 1860, members of the public donated about 600 volumes to its long-standing library, and in the same year a Public Library and Reading Room established at Tulbagh carried a German newspaper, as well as others in English from Natal and the 'Frontier'. It also commenced a series of lectures for the benefit of the library and the community. In 1871, there was a similar amalgamation at Bredasdorp, and, by 1875, many book and reading societies had transformed themselves into, or

colony, Mauritius, Belgium, and Hong Kong. The United States was the second largest source of printed books, followed by Germany until the mid 1890s. Books imported from Holland overtook both Germany and the United States by 1898, and continued to rise.

amalgamated with, government-funded public libraries. The older Aliwal North Reading Association merged with the Aliwal North Public Library in 1873. It donated its Reading Room, books, newspapers, and periodicals on the condition that the Association's remaining ten members would be exempted from library subscription fees for the first year.[30] This public library had been active in 1860, but required resuscitation in August 1870, and again in April 1872.[31] When the library was inactive, the town's newspaper rallied public support for it as a necessary institution to avoid the charges of being a 'non-reading or illiterate community', and of 'not promoting literary activities'.[32]

Shared Spaces, Literacy Levels, and 'the Literary'

At that time, 'literary' had the basic educational meaning of using literature to improve literacy skills. This was necessary in the Aliwal North district of the Cape Colony where literacy levels had hardly changed in a decade. In 1865, only 10.34 per cent in a total population of 21,785 residents could read and write. By 1875, the figure was 7.8 per cent in a population of 29,344 residents, and the majority of Blacks were unable to read or write (*Results of a Census*, 1877, p. 57). The Aliwal North Reading Association's amalgamation with the library and a successful application for an annual government grant were therefore significant developments. This Association had formerly called itself a Reading Club, and its 1873 catalogue of items donated to the library listed popular and literary periodicals such as *Athenaeum*, *Atlantic Monthly*, *Cornhill Magazine*, and *Edinburgh Review*, as well as the *Cape Monthly Magazine*, and other titles in German and Dutch. The library's impressive section on natural and applied science books can probably be attributed to its exceptional librarian for about forty years. His name was Alfred 'Gogga' Brown and he had a large private collection. He had been a member of the Reading Association, and as an autodidact, he

---

[30] *Replies to Circular, 1873–4*, CO 4692, Cape Archives Depot.

[31] *Aliwal Observer and Dordrecht and Lady Grey Times*, 20 August 1870.

[32] *Aliwal North Standard and Basutoland, Lady Grey and Dordrecht Register*, 20 April 1872.

was variously a schoolteacher, a postmaster, and an amateur palaeontologist (Drennan, 1900, p. 81).

Like reading societies, literary societies and mutual improvement societies also provided reading spaces, and some began as joint ventures with public libraries in small towns. This was the case with the Ceres Public Library and Mutual Improvement Society in 1860.[33] Others collaborated with public libraries. About 100 kilometres south east of Ceres, the town of Robertson established its Mutual Improvement Society in October 1883. It served as a forum for exchanging knowledge for the benefit of its English and Dutch-speaking members (Lewis, 1987). This society was a debating space as well as a reading space. It used alternate Tuesday evening meetings for members to read and discuss self-prepared written essays on any subject except theological matters. The Robertson Public Library, established in 1872, advertised its proceedings and the Society's members used the library resources to prepare essays and debates, confirming their close relationship.

The Society's debates and essays dealt with contemporary themes. In December 1883, an essay at one of the meetings asked the question: 'Ought the Aborigines of this country to be educated on the same platform as the Colonists?' The question for debate at a meeting in January 1884 was: 'Is it expedient that the Franchise of this Colony should be raised?' Literary topics included 'Folk Lore', 'The History of Words', and 'Robert Burns'. And literary debates asked whether 'the study of the Classics or of Science is best calculated to develop the mind', and 'Does poetry decline as civilization advances?' In 1905, the Society's name changed to the Robertson Literary Society, and it admitted women as members.[34] Other countryside voluntary societies adopted similar programmes and patterns of activity. By the 1890s some of them were called literary and debating societies, such as the Alma Literary and Debating Society in Kimberley (1897–1903). Its improving magazine, '*The Alma Terroriser*', included literary contributions from

---

[33] Cape Archives, Ampt Pubs, CCP1/2/1/9, A56. It became the Ceres Public Library in 1883.

[34] It is still active today and presents an annual 'Stakesby Lewis' lecture in honour of one of its founding members. https://rivertonstud.co.za/heritage/history-of-robertson/. Accessed 21 November 2019.

members.[35] Literary and debating societies were active also in Cape Town, Johannesburg, Pretoria, and Bloemfontein, and the smaller towns of the Natal Colony (see Appendix).

Several voluntary societies collaborated with each other and with the public libraries to stimulate cultural and intellectual growth, and to provide entertainment in small towns and settlements. Annual government grants and membership fees were the principal sources of income for the public libraries, and they arranged lectures as well as literary and musical entertainments to raise revenue. When the grant was still £100, Grahamstown Public Library, for example, raised over £1,000 for the period 1864–72, and Graaff-Reinet Public Library made just over £50 for the period 1867–9. Together, these countryside public libraries and other voluntary societies expanded the range of reading spaces and types of literature for readers.

Conclusion

Through the efforts of readers and reading communities, reading spaces evolved from family and religious settings into secular voluntary societies in a spirit of improvement in South Africa's small towns and settlements. In the second half of the nineteenth century, reading communities used these societies to negotiate the country's special mix of language, cultural, and religious identities through skilful political and literary engagement. A discussion of the origins, programmes, and legacies of English literary societies, Dutch-Afrikaans debating societies, and African mutual improvement societies in the next Section throws more light on these reading communities and their reading programmes.

2 Reading, Writing, Debating, Reciting

Megan Voss (2012, p. 22) argues that the foundations of Queenstown as a settler-colonial town were framed in 1853 by a rhetoric of improvement that emphasised 'English notions of education, rights and progress [which imposed] a cultural construct onto a barren, neutral landscape'. She explains that this ignored the fact that before settlement the landscape was far from

---

[35] *The Alma Terroriser*, Kimberley Africana Library, M 53.

empty. The rich culture of the aba-Thembu and the rock art of the San of the Eastern Cape region were simply overlooked to create a new ethos and network of intellectuals in the town. Its library, museum, and mutual improvement society were key institutions to achieve this improvement. A proposal in 1865 for a literary institute explained that it would get 'the rough edges of the townsman's character taken off by ... having access to a healthy and improving class of literary productions' (Voss, 2012, p. 40). As in Queenstown, this rhetoric would be defended, challenged, and changed in English literary societies, Dutch-Afrikaans debating societies, and African mutual improvement societies in small towns and settlements in the second half of the nineteenth century. In these societies, reading communities adapted ideas of improvement to serve other cultural and political purposes.

Swellendam Literary Institute

Established in 1830, the Swellendam Book Society was renamed the Swellendam Reading Society in 1852. It then became the Swellendam Literary Institute and eventually merged with the Swellendam Public Library for financial reasons. This library had itself been established in 1838, and the local cricket club and agricultural society often rented it for their meetings. This space was used on occasion to discuss topics of general interest, such as a public meeting on education in May 1862. Like the Book and Reading Societies before it, the Literary Institute members also met in the library. In its lifespan of about eight years, divergent views of literary value in a culture of improvement became apparent in a town that was diverse in its population and language. Of the 2,009 residents (925 European and 1084 'Coloured') in 1865, there were 776 or 38.62 per cent who could read and write in either English, Dutch, or German.[36] The Institute's members were, however, primarily English-speaking, and its lectures and readings intended to bring 'rational amusement' to Swellendam.

An elitist outlook complicated efforts to attract the general public and to collaborate with the town's other voluntary societies. 'Mr. Russouw' of

---

[36] *Overberg Courant*, 29 March 1865. 'Coloured' was used in the 1865 census as a collective noun for those named as 'Hottentot', 'Kafir', and 'Other'.

a local Young Men's Improvement Society, who had been invited to read an essay on '*The acquired qualities of the mind,*' was accused of plagiarism. Several letters to the *Overberg Courant*'s editor ensued, presenting different views of the incident. The chairperson should not have criticised the young man to his face, wrote one correspondent, adding that other Institute lectures were compilations too instead of originals. But the newspaper editor, who claimed to have attended some meetings of that Improvement Society, confirmed that the speaker had not composed a single sentence. He advised the speaker and other young men that 'the public will not recognise a bold and presumptuous bearing, without ordinary intelligence, as indication of genius'.[37] It mattered little that English was probably not the speaker's first language. Nor that the Improvement Society may have considered the successful public reading of an essay more important than who its author was. Whether it had been copied was less significant for non-English speakers than improving one's elocution skills, deemed especially valuable for debating in an English colony.[38]

At that time, the Dutch Reformed Church was establishing mutual improvement societies in the colony. Reverend Andrew Murray had started one in Cape Town where a young Jan Hendrik Hofmeyr[39] and other Dutch speakers were members. Its proceedings were in English, and debates included the use and abuse of novels, as well as the power of the press (Hofmeyr & Reitz, 1913, p. 65). The Literary Institute's relation with mutual improvement societies was still strained five years later. Another invited lecture, this time to promote the formation of these societies, again proved controversial. Dr Antoine Changuion, a liberal-minded and internationally respected Dutch linguist, was accused of using this opportunity to raise funds to support cleric Reverend Thomas Burgers' heresy case in the Cape Supreme Court.[40] Steering away from church and language politics, several lectures

---

[37] Mr Russouw's 'Lecture', *Overberg Courant*, 24 August 1860.

[38] Lovedale Missionary Institute, for example, ran elocution competitions (Hofmeyr, 2006, p. 272).

[39] He became a well-known politician and newspaper editor.

[40] *Overberg Courant*, 25 January 1865. Burgers, who later became the President of the South African Republic, was also chairperson of the Hanover Public Library.

and readings were, however, presented at the Institute's meetings. A selection was published in 1862 under the title *Literary Recreations*. Printed by Pike & Byles and advertised as Swellendam's first locally produced book, it claimed to say 'much for the public spirit of the inhabitants'.[41] It had hoped to prove that 'even in the wilds of South Africa' audiences appreciated literary pleasures.

Besides essays of historical and scientific interest, there were literary contributions on 'The Words We Use', 'Scott and His Poetry', 'The Influences of Nature and Literature', and Archdeacon Nathaniel Merriman's lecture on the study of Shakespeare.[42] Reverend J. Baker's chapter on his 'Literary Reminiscences' is a condescending view of books and reading. He argued that in a country like South Africa, unlike older countries like England where 'the minds of people generally are more disciplined', guidance in reading is of 'the greatest importance as affecting the growth of a national character' (Baker, 1862, p. 93). That is why, he argued, to learn the world as it is in works of fiction, 'Dickens, Bulwer, Kingsley, and Disraeli' are to be preferred to Frederick Marryat and James Fenimore Cooper[43] and others of their class which should only be 'taken occasionally, as one goes for a ride in the country' (Baker, 1862, p. 107). The Reverend's 'preferred' authors were probably among the books that the Literary Institute donated in 1870 to the Swellendam Public Library.

The wider reading preferences in Swellendam were quite different, however, from that of the Institute. A library subcommittee reported in that same year that 111 volumes of 'Tales' or light fiction were 'still unaccounted for'.[44] And the novels auctioned from time to time in the library's Reading Room generously supplemented the library's income from annual government grants and subscription fees. The Institute's

---

[41] *Overberg Courant*, 17 September 1862.

[42] He had delivered two lectures on Shakespeare at a 'General Institute' in Grahamstown in 1857 (Wright, 2008).

[43] Their books were listed in the catalogues of several rural public libraries.

[44] *Report of the Sub-Committee appointed at the meeting held in the Library on the 19th August 1870 to consider the best means of resuscitating the Institution*, Swellendam Archives.

lectures and public readings were advertised and reviewed regularly in the *Overberg Courant*, which was read and circulated also in nearby towns. But this newspaper included material that appealed to Swellendam's working classes. In March 1863, it published 'The Poor Washerwoman' from the improving magazine, *The British Workman*. This piece's language did not differ much from that of the more literary *Cornhill Magazine*, and assumed that there were intelligent readers among the working classes. The *Overberg Courant* also summarised the proceedings of annual meetings of library subscribers, and periodically announced the addition of new titles to the library's catalogue.[45]

Through its own programme of lectures, the Swellendam Public Library supported a popular focus that the Institute overlooked. It allowed its Reading Room to remain open for two hours in the evening to offer 'agreeable and useful recreation to all classes'.[46] There were special concessions for country subscribers, such as permission to borrow more books for longer periods. And Penny Readings in the winter months attracted the working classes. In this way, the library both challenged and complemented the work of the Literary Institute. Some Institute speakers in turn used the library's books for their lectures, and, in July 1864, it encouraged young men who attended a public reading of Dickens' *A Christmas Carol* to become library members.[47] Institute members even donated their colonial newspapers to the library for the benefit of poorer readers. The well-known Afrikaans prose writer M. E. Rothmann wrote that English historian James Anthony Froude warmly complimented the library collection during a visit (Rothmann, 1947, p. 68).[48]

The Literary Institute was, however, in terminal decline by the mid 1860s as a result of a drop in its membership after the Montague and Robertson field cornetcies were separated from Swellendam. But

---

[45] *Overberg Courant*, 17 August 1864; 2 November 1864.

[46] *Overberg Courant*, 30 September 1863; 14 October 1863.

[47] *Overberg Courant*, 15 June 1864; 27 July 1864.

[48] She also acknowledged this library's role in her own literary career (Immelman, 1970, p. 76).

controversy persisted with the reading of Alfred Tennyson's narrative poem *Enoch Arden*, advertised as 'An Evening with Tennyson at Swellendam'. The reader, Honourable J. C. Davidson who was also the Cape Colony's Treasurer-General, was criticised in a letter to the *Courant*. His elocution was described as 'slip-shod, mamby-pamby, and mumble-jumble'. Another letter argued that this was all jealousy from a rival reader 'whose Swellendam reputation Mr Davidson has snuffed out'.[49] Ending, however, on a gender-progressive, if controversial, note, the Literary Institute announced in May 1865 a reading by 'Mrs Hutchinson . . . a lady of education and accomplishment'.[50] Just a few years later, similar complexities and contradictions surfaced in the Wodehouse Literary Society, about 870 km north east of Swellendam.

Wodehouse Literary Society

In the Dordrecht area of the Eastern Cape in the early 1870s, a library too was a part of the Wodehouse Literary Society, but as one of its subcommittees. It supported the Society's programmes that included debates, lectures, readings in dramatic and general literature, as well as musical entertainments. Andrew Gontshi probably became the first Black South African officially appointed as a librarian when the Society elected him for this position in 1874.[51] The committee skills honed in this capacity would prepare him for leadership roles in political associations that he later helped to establish. Gontshi had been educated at the Lovedale Institution, and had probably been a member too of the Lovedale Literary Society and the Lovedale Public Library.

Reverend Andrew Smith, a teacher there at that time, reported that the young men of the institution both worked under superintendence and used this library. A new catalogue was printed every time that a case of books arrived. Smith believed that the 'abundance of opinion and intelligence in the home country' (England) would stimulate the reading tastes of 'native young men', which were 'evidently growing rapidly'.[52] They, however,

[49] *Overberg Courant*, 15 March 1865; 22 March 1865.
[50] *Overberg Courant*, 3 May 1865. [51] *Cape Argus*, 24 February 1874.
[52] *Replies to Circular, 1873–4*, CO 4692, Cape Archives.

applied their skills in unexpected ways, and Gontshi subsequently founded the Association for the Advancement of the Ngqika, and the Union for Native Opinion (Odendaal, 1993, p. 9). It must have been a challenge for Gontshi to grow a Black membership for the Wodehouse Literary Society and its library. By 1875, there were still only seventy-one male and fifty-six female Wodehouse residents 'Other than European or White' who could read.[53]

But some of those who could read became members of this Society. Its programme for June to October 1873 included debates on free trade; federation; the superiority of Napoleon as General; and Dutch versus English laws of inheritance. There was also a lecture on the advantages of a Cape university to the colony, as well as several public readings and recitations. A Cape Town newspaper reporting on the Wodehouse Literary Society stated that 'For a country village in South Africa this programme indicates a great deal of intellectual life in the locality, and it would be well if other places were to follow the example of Dordrecht'.[54] This certainly happened, and neighbouring towns added debating programmes to form literary and debating societies (see Appendix). And their connections with reading and libraries remained key features.

Whereas the English-language literary and debating societies had middle-class memberships and emphasised their cultural importance, the Dutch-Afrikaans and African-language voluntary societies that emerged would stress their 'improving' educational and political roles. Becoming 'literary' for them meant self-improvement through the mastery of the basic literacy skills of speaking, reading, and writing in their own languages. It also implied agency and self-determination through participation in the political changes unfolding in South Africa. These voluntary societies were viewed by their members as people's universities and political schools (van der Bank, 1993; Odendaal, 2012).

---

[53] Results of a Census of the Colony of the Cape of Good Hope. Cape Town: Saul Solomon, 1877, p. 74.

[54] *Cape Argus*, 22 July 1873.

Dutch-Afrikaans Debating Societies

From about the 1870s, Dutch-Afrikaans Debating Societies raised literary, cultural, and political awareness in remote rural towns such as Komga-Diepkloof, Vlekpoort, and Bruintjieshoogte. Typically named Young People's Debating Societies or just Debating Societies, they were valuable too for a literary self-education (Booyens, 1983, p. 12; Marais, 2009, p. 85). Their cultural importance cannot be underestimated, and the Biesiesvlei Debating Society was considered this little town's 'first taste of culture' (Conradie, 1985). South African poets A. G. Visser, Cornelis J. Langenhoven, and Eugene N. Marais were active members of these societies, as were the novelists D. F. Malherbe and J. van Bruggen. Langenhoven (1914, p. 71), who was a member of the Oudtshoorn Debating Society and wrote a guidebook for use by other societies, described them as 'grindstones' in post-school days where one's thinking may be purposefully sharpened.[55] Importantly, these societies kept manuscript journals that recorded their members' original literary contributions such as essays, poems, dialogues, plays, short stories, and letters to the journal editor recorded in Dutch, Dutch-Afrikaans, and English.

They spread quickly across the countryside. There were two types, and the secular societies differed from the religious societies, which affiliated with the Dutch Reformed Church and drew on Western European models.[56] Some, like Oudtshoorn's secular society, on the other hand, had evolved from the town's Mutual Improvement Society (Booyens, 1983, p. 39). Subsequently called the Oudtshoorn Parliamentary Debating Society, it featured contemporary political and economic topics. Ironically, it was the town's religious debating society that first admitted women. There were more similarities than differences between the two types, and historical events consolidated their political and cultural missions. The First Anglo-Boer war (1880–1) and the South African war (1899–1902) deepened a political and cultural consciousness among Afrikaners, and reawakened an

---

[55] Another guide with examples was van der Spuy, 1913. As a student at the University of Stellenbosch, Langenhoven had also been a member of its Union Debating Society.

[56] These were the Christian Youth and Debating Societies.

interest in language and literary developments. Whereas Dutch and English were not unusual in the proceedings of some societies, the Afrikaans language featured prominently after these wars.[57] This was, however, not the rule, and from its inception in 1876 until 1890, English was dominant at Stellenbosch's Union Debating Society. After that, Dutch was preferred until 1918, when Afrikaans was entrenched.

From early on, it was customary for debates and meetings to be conducted in Afrikaans, while Dutch remained the dominant language for the speeches, lectures, written pieces, and official matters. The minutes of the Stanford Debating Society in the Overberg region, for example, only switched to Afrikaans in 1921 (Booyens, 1983, p. 72). Although divergent interests thwarted attempts to unify these societies, political decisions to achieve the Union of South Africa in 1910 spurred this process. Religious-oriented societies led the way, and the Cape Union of Christian Young Peoples' Debating Societies was launched in 1904 in Cape Town. It had ninety-four affiliated branches by 1910, representing 3,185 members. A similar Union of the several religious-oriented debating societies in the Transvaal or South African Republic was established in Boksburg in 1906. It represented about fifty branches by 1914, and had a combined membership of about 2,000 by 1918 (Booyens, 1983, p. 64).

By the time that the Union of Natal Debating Societies was launched in 1917, Afrikaans had become the preferred language for many of its member societies.[58] Afrikaans had already unified the religious-oriented societies in the Orange Free State republic (subsequently the Orange River colony), where military and nationalist elements typified their pattern of development. Here Dutch Reformed Ministers connected with the Afrikaner Bond[59] had nurtured an Afrikaner ethnic consciousness, and elaborated an

---

[57] At a Debating Society in a detention camp in Ceylon, Paul Roux submitted a poem, 'Myn Moedertaal', that preferred Afrikaans over Dutch (Brink, 1960).

[58] The first Debating and Literary Society in Natal was established in Pietermaritzburg in February 1908 (Prinsloo, 1995). A bilingual Dutch–English one was active at the Transvaal University College (University of Pretoria), in the same year.

[59] The Afrikaner Bond was a political organisation founded in 1880.

ethnic culture (Giliomee, 1991, p. 41). They added a programme of shoot-ing skills, and revived commemorations of the Battle of Blood River[60] as standard features in their annual programmes. By 1907 their societies, some with as many as eighty members each, had become instruments in the Afrikaner cultural struggle, and promoted Christian National education (Nienaber, 1947, pp. 23–35).

Secular societies also sought to amalgamate, and to accommodate reli-gious societies. As a result, the Central Union of Debating and Christian Young People's Societies in the Cape was launched in 1889, curiously in Murraysburg, a predominantly Afrikaans-speaking 'Coloured' town. But its motto 'Knowledge and Development' soon changed to 'Forward Afrikaners' to signal a political shift (Booyens, 1983, p. 48). The cue for this development may have come from the prominent Union Debating Society in Stellenbosch where the statement 'the Colony derives no benefit from the Higher Education of Natives' had won by 16 votes to 0 (Na Vyftig Jaar, 1926, p. 36). In the Transvaal, about fifteen independent or secular societies assumed an increasingly Afrikaans and racially exclusive character and remained active until the Second World War.

Although debating featured prominently in these societies' programmes, the members' literary contributions were equally if not more intriguing. These were recorded by elected 'journalists' in the societies' manuscript journals, several of which are still preserved today in church and other archives around the country.[61] Literacy and 'the literary' intersected in these societies, and the evaluation and critique of written pieces mattered as much as the mastery of reading, writing, and speaking. Public readings of original essays tested and improved the art of reading rather than simply acquiring knowledge. For several years, the *Volksleesboek*, and, ironically, *The Royal Path of Life*, provided topics and source material for members.

The 'essay' as another programme item tested the art of original composition and creative writing. Uncertainty and anxiety in the years before Union, the importance of preserving their histories and language, as

---

[60] Originally known as Dingaan's Day, this was the name given to the battle between the Voortrekkers and the Zulus on 16 December, 1838.

[61] Journals were kept separate from the minute books.

well as prospects of employment in new administrative positions may have led to essays on 'The Archives in Cape Town', 'Our Language', and 'The Politics of our State'. In a few cases, the journals carried essays copied or '*overgenomen*' from other sources that had been read aloud and critiqued by members. If judged worthy of inclusion by the 'journalists' at the monthly or bi-monthly 'Journal nights', the essays would be copied into the Society's magazine by the 'journalists' or their assistants.

The standard programme of the secular Klein Drakenstein Debating Society, active in the Cape's Paarl region from 1891 to the 1920s, comprised a debate, a reading or essay, and a recitation, although a '*vrije-woord*' or open topic was not unusual. The names of members responsible for the following meeting's items, as well as the topic of the next debate along with the 'opener' and 'opposer' were usually announced at the end of each monthly meeting.[62] Klein Drakenstein's journal included English poems such as the ballad *Death of Jan Cronje* and H. W. Longfellow's *The Wreck of the Hesperus*.[63] An intriguing poem about Cecil John Rhodes appears in the journal of the secular *Dicendo Discimus* Debating Society in Pretoria. Entitled '*The political death and burial of Cecil John*', the opening lines are:

> Who killed Cecil John? 'I', said the Ballot Act,
> 'All thro' his want o' tact, I killed Cecil John.'
> Who saw him die? 'I', said the Bond,[64]
> 'Of him once so fond, I saw him die.'[65]

But this society's journals for 1896 to 1898, which run to more than 300 pages and contain 110 literary contributions, intended primarily to develop

---

[62] A type of spreadsheet in the back of the minute book shows how names and responsibilities were rotated.

[63] Klein Drakenstein Debating Society, Cape Archives, ZD/K2.

[64] A reference to the Afrikaner Bond.

[65] *Dicendo Discimus*, Joernaal der Debatsvereniging, University of Pretoria Library, A10, Book 1, p. 46. Rhodes drove the Franchise and Ballot Act of 1892 that disenfranchised a large number of non-white, as well as poor-white, voters.

and maintain the Dutch language. At the Magaliesberg Debating Society near Pretoria where Dutch was also favoured, the aims were to develop both literary knowledge and oratorical skills, and several journal entries ended with the phrase, 'Ik heb gezegd' (I have spoken). It was established in 1898, and its journal was so treasured that it lay buried for eight months during the South African War.[66] By 1917, in another town and with an amended name, this Society was still active with the help of Langenhoven's guidebook. Readings now addressed labour strikes and women's right to vote, and the journal included short stories, dialogues, and other literary items.

About 300 kilometres east of Magaliesburg, the Boven Vallei Debating and Dramatic Society enjoyed an equally active literary programme that carried Dutch and English items.[67] Its monthly journal programme dates from 1903 and members submitted essays, poems, short stories, and dialogues or short sketches that were often performed, adding an exciting dimension to proceedings. The Boven Vallei journal editors appealed for original contributions, and provided useful tips for writers. In one case, an original submission and a corrected version in the journal shows all the editorial changes. This practice demonstrates the adult literacy and literary functions that these societies performed in remote locations. The annual 'Public Entertainments' of some societies included musical and dramatic performances to raise funds, which they used to extend their educational reach to the general public. Their reports in local newspapers and journals amplified their impact across Dutch-Afrikaans communities from the 1870s until the early decades of the twentieth century.

Several debating societies established libraries in small country towns, assisted, in some instances, by the supply of crates of Dutch books from the Algemeen Nederlands Verbond's 'Boekencommissie' in Rotterdam from 1903 onwards.[68] Debates and essays on the value of books and reading in

---

[66] Argief van die Magaliesberg Nasionale Debatsvereniging, National Archives, Pretoria, A 1026.

[67] Debat en Dramatisch Vereeniging Boven Vallei, Wits Historical Papers, A203.

[68] Cape Archives, Algemeen Nederlands Verbond, A1545/AG 8397–8. The value of imported Dutch books to South Africa for 1903 was second highest after the UK with £11812, and continued to surpass other countries in that decade.

their programmes, as well as the supply of literature in Dutch, Afrikaans, and English strengthened a reading culture across rural South Africa.

African Mutual Improvement Societies

Reading spaces for political and 'literary' education expanded too in African-language reading communities in the 1880s. Ironically, the Afrikaner Bond inspired this development. In 1882, Simon Sihlali, a leader of the *Imbumba Yama Nyama*[69] (the South African Aborigines Association), asked 'Where is our Bond?', and by the next year there were over 300 *Imbumba* members with branches in Port Elizabeth, Graaff-Reinet, and Colesberg (Odendaal, 2012, pp. 68, 70). Several types of associations and societies sought to address political, social, and educational challenges but urban–rural, clan, language, class, and other divisions complicated their longevity and effectiveness. Also, much of their activity was reported in vernacular newspapers and not readily accessible to outsiders. Some of the associations and societies, however, attempted to bridge these divides, and their activities across the countryside reveal concerted efforts at improvement across South Africa. In Northern Cape settlements, groups of illiterate Africans used to gather around local ministers, school teachers, or younger readers to hear about essayist, novelist, and poet John Dube, and about political activist and newspaper editor John Tengo Jabavu.

Sol Plaatje (1916, p. 5) recalls reading newspapers (probably the English–isiXhosa *Imvo Zabatsundu* and the Setswana-language *Mahoko a Becwana*) aloud as a boy 'under the shady trees outside the cattle fold' at Pniel mission station near Barkly West.[70] This practice stimulated 'the interest in politics amongst Africans of all classes' (Odendaal, 1984, p. 63). When *Mahoko a Becwana*, for example, reported in 1893 that Cecil Rhodes intended to gain control of Bechuanaland, a missionary observed 'several leading men of the town [Kanye] sitting as solemn as a congregation of owls around a copy of the newspaper' (Words of Batswana, 2006, p. xxix).

---

[69] Loosely, it means solid unity or unity is strength.

[70] This happened in the early 1890s when literacy had not improved much from the 9.09 per cent rate at this mission station in 1849 (Fourie et al., 2013, p. 26).

Mahoko also published Moffat Institution senior student Ntloyatshipi Pula's three-part commentary on Setswana proverbs, and his regular column on 'Things That Are Not Known'. Anxiety about retaining their land, and control of their language and indigenous knowledge, stimulated political and literary discussions and debates in the Batswana community. Besides religious matters, letter writers to *Mahoko* discussed the benefits and challenges of education, books, and reading, as well as disagreements with editors (Volz, 2007). This pattern was found wherever 'the literary' and the encouragement to read carried a political purpose (Odendaal, 2012, p. 57).

At the Lovedale Literary Society in the 1880s, divergent meanings of 'literary', 'reading', and 'debating' emerged among teachers and students. For teachers, literature was a moralising force that would 'improve' readers and 'save' them from 'corrupting pastimes' (Hofmeyr, 2006: 266). For students, literature had become less important than debating because debating was about training for leadership. Students maintained that literature should serve political purposes and 'current events, be they local or national' (Hofmeyr, 2006: 269). As a result, quotations from Shakespeare, Dickens, and Scott would be used in political speeches nurtured in student debates. This shift reflected broader political and economic developments in the region. Whereas Africans in the Eastern Cape in the early 1870s had adapted in 'all spheres ... to the Cape Colony's institutions, systems, and norms', this began to change as a consequence of mineral discoveries and further wars and setbacks in the late 1870s (Odendaal, 2012: 39–40). Disillusionment spread among educated adult Africans at this time, and was felt by their children at missionary schools.

The promise of a bright future dimmed at the Presbyterian Lovedale Institution, as well as the Methodist Healdtown and Clarkebury schools. This happened too at the Anglican Zonnebloem College in Cape Town, and the Anglican Institution in Grahamstown. Alumni of these institutions responded by initiating a network of African-led voluntary associations. By the 1880s and 1890s, these associations helped to 'improve' fellow Africans and to safeguard their political rights. They included Vigilance Associations, Native Associations, Educational Associations, and *Manyanos* or Political Associations, as well as Mutual Improvement Associations or Societies. In the Native Education Association, Paul Xiniwe read an essay in January 1884 arguing that it was time for Africans to sit in Parliament (Odendaal, 2012, p. 62). The programmes of mutual improvement associations began to blend political and literary themes. They were familiar in African communities where missionary societies established some themselves. In 1889, for example, the Wesleyan Methodists started one in Knysna (Whiteside, 1906, p. 156).

In African hands, they pressed for political mobilisation. But because they were not reported in the English colonial press, their activities were largely unknown. Vernacular newspapers, however, introduced a generation that was breaking free from 'the Victorians' conception of themselves as the leaders of civilisation' who had produced Shakespeare, Bacon, and Milton (Odendaal, 2012, pp. 61–2). This generation would produce Sol Plaatje, Samuel Mqhayi, John Dube, and Robert Grendon. Lovedale graduates helped to establish the Burnshill Young Men's Mutual Improvement Association and the D'Urban Teachers' Mutual Improvement Association, and Healdtown had its own association. Topics such as the registration of Africans as voters were discussed, and members were expected to read newspapers and become familiar with public affairs. Mutual improvement associations were also started in Port Elizabeth, and, in 1884, there was one in Butterworth (Gcuwa, and later called the Transkei Mutual Improvement Association).

Mission-educated Africans from the Eastern Cape who found jobs in Kimberley in the 1880s and 1890s, were prominent in that city's network of clubs and societies. The South Africans Improvement Society typified 'their ideals and aspirations', and the name avoided 'Native' or 'African' to emphasise 'nationality rather than race' as a defining factor of identity (Willan, 1984, p. 36). Described as 'non-political and un-denominational', it was established in June 1895, and emphasised cultivating the use of the English language and criticism in readings, recitations, and composition. Performance of musical selections were included too in some programmes. Sol Plaatje's 'literary debut' as a member was a reading of Max O'Rell's *John Bull and Co*. The secretary, Simon Mokuena, reported that the reading was 'fairly criticised' and that 'the mistakes corrected did not only benefit the reader, but also the other members'.[71] Plaatje probably mocked the reference to John Bull as Britain acting in the interest of South Africa as a whole, when in fact it meant the interests of the English and Dutch-Afrikaners to 'maintain white supremacy against the Africans' (Giliomee, 1991, p. 40).

At the same meeting, the recitation by Walter Kawa of Milton's *Paradise Lost* was recorded by Mokuena as 'not highly appreciated by the majority of members, as it was too classical to be comprehended by the average native mind'. Willan (1984, p. 37) argues that this was an example of overstepping 'the limits of social and literary one-upmanship', and of Mokuena's doubts about the universality and comprehensibility of English culture. At another meeting devoted to short essays, Plaatje read one that he composed called 'The History of the Bechuanas'.[72] 'Being a Bechuana by birth, he showed great mastery over his subject', according to Mokuena. A West African member, W. Cowen, also read an essay that he composed on 'Civilisation and Its Advantages for the African Races'. The Society encouraged the composition of essays as original and creative pieces of writing, and as part of its aim of promoting a literary education. Mokuena's essay on 'Reading', for example, was described as having been delivered in a humorous style that 'made his paper interesting'.

Membership of this society encouraged Plaatje to read after office hours in his post office job in Kimberley. As a young boy, he had already purchased his own books from money earned as a groom at a hotel near the Pniel mission station. In Kimberley, he may well have used the public library's concession of free visitor access to its reading room. The average daily attendance of visitors at the Kimberley Public Library rose from 166 in 1894 when he arrived in the town to 285 when he left for Mafeking in 1898.[73] Also intended to be a Debating Society, topics in the South Africans Improvement Society broached controversial issues regarding

---

[71] *Diamond Fields Advertiser*, 23 August 1895. This newspaper published the Society's reports.

[72] Ibid. Not to be mistaken for A. J. Wookey's *History of the Bechuana*.

[73] Called Mahikeng today; Reports of Public Libraries, *Cape of Good Hope Blue Books/Statistical Register*, 1894 and 1898.

'civilised life', such as: 'Is lobola[74] as practised at the present time justifiable?' Defending the negative view, even if it contradicted private convictions, improved an individual member's qualities of critique and resistance. Mass resistance, on the other hand, characterised the Becoana Mutual Improvement Society at Thaba 'Nchu, about 500 kilometres south-east of Mafeking. With about 25,000 Sotho and Tswana-speaking members, it was a powerful political player in the Orange River Colony in the years leading up to the Union of South Africa.

Reverend Joel Goronyane, a Lovedale graduate and Wesleyan minister who helped to establish it in about 1899, was well-acquainted with the educational value of such societies. Prominent leaders of the Baralong people had assisted Goronyane in attempts to unify African and Coloured organisations, and to negotiate with key national intermediaries (Odendaal, 1984, pp. 158, 168). The Becoana Mutual Improvement Society was seen as 'one of the strongest bases' of the fledgling South African Native Convention (which Goronyane chaired) during the desperate but failed efforts to include Africans in the Union Government in 1910 (Odendaal, 2012, pp. 439–41). He was also a member of the Thaba 'Nchu syndicate that launched *Tsala ea Becoana* (*The Bechuana Friend*), which Plaatje edited. This English–Tswana newspaper with a circulation of several thousand would provide an effective African voice in the new Whites-only Union of South Africa. By that time, as Opland (2003, p. 40) aptly states, 'print media introduced by whites had been conscripted in the struggle for political and social equality'.

Conclusion

In the 1870s and 1880s, Dutch-Afrikaans debating societies and African-language mutual improvement societies evinced a shift in the 'English' rhetoric of improvement that typified the voluntary societies of Queenstown, Swellendam, and Wodehouse. In other towns and settlements, political and economic developments had also thrown into sharp relief the realities and consequences of English cultural domination. Dutch-Afrikaner debating societies responded by affirming language rights and cultural expression to present alternative ways of political participation. In

---

[74] Bride price, traditionally paid with cattle.

their turn, African mutual improvement societies adapted literacy and literary activities to produce alternative political strategies. Through their own voluntary societies, Dutch-Afrikaner and Black reading communities reframed the 'English' rhetoric and ethos of improvement, and stressed ideas about education, rights, and equality. Reframing did not, however, mean rejecting, and the remarkable reception of the works of Charles Dickens demonstrated some of the complexities of South Africans' literary engagement with Victorian literature.

3 Dickens on the Page, the Podium, and the Stage

Activists found political value in reading Charles Dickens' works during South Africa's liberation struggle (Cope, 1950; Dick, 2012). But from about the mid nineteenth to early twentieth centuries they mattered more for cultural and literary reasons, as well as for recreation and entertainment in town and countryside. Early acquisitions by the South African Public Library are *Sketches by Boz* in 1837, followed by *Oliver Twist* and *Pickwick Papers* in 1839. And *Martin Chuzzlewit*, which was added in 1844, is listed too in 1846 as 'incomplete' in a Cape Town Police library catalogue.[75] Reading Dickens in parts was not unusual then. His popularity grew when Cape newspaper owners, in their efforts to survive financially, serialised fresh instalments of his works since the early 1840s – usually without permission.[76] They may have taken advantage of the practice in Britain where, since the early nineteenth century, greater frequency of magazines like the monthly *Blackwood's* had made possible the serialisation of popular fiction that would appear later in books.[77] This made fiction more accessible and affordable than buying the subsequent first editions (Brake, 2017).

[75] *Supplementary Catalogues of the South African Public Library* for 1837, 1839, and 1844; *Cape Town Police Library*, Item 208, p. 10. *Chuzzlewit* was probably serialised in episodes in an English literary magazine.

[76] In New Zealand, *Little Dorrit* and *Our Mutual Friend* were also serialised in mid-nineteenth-century newspapers; see Traue, 2016, p. 148.

[77] *Macmillan's Magazine* was, for example, identified with Thomas Hughes' Tom Brown's School Days at Port Elizabeth Public Library, 'Our Library Table', *Eastern Province Magazine*, 1 (1), 1861, p. 32.

On the Page

Dickens' characters became 'a common factor of interest and conversation between readers of different classes and walks of life' (Varley, 1958, p. 21). They were family entertainment and family gossip. Sergeant Buzfuz and Augustus Snodgrass of *Pickwick Papers* became well known through the pages of the *Cape Town Mail and Mirror of Court and Council* in 1841. And a few years later, the *South African Commercial Advertiser* published chapters of *The Chimes* reputedly 'without prejudice . . . to the copyright, but rather as a kind of advertisement'.[78] As in other parts of the world, if the mail steamers that ferried these chapters across the oceans did not arrive on schedule, 'there was the added tension of delight postponed'. Dickens 'came to speak *to* and even *for* an entirely new reading public on a far-flung scale', and 'made the novel respectable' at the Cape (Varley, 1958, p. 21–2).

Even Dutch translations were popular in working class suburbs. In a library of 6,008 books at the Salt River Institute in 1906, eighteen of the forty-nine Dutch titles were Dickens' works, among which were *Grote verwachtingen*, *Kleine Dora*, and *Dombey en Zoon* (Paterson & Bryant, 1906, p. 58). Complete works were also available for sale, and when parts of *David Copperfield* enclosed in muddy-blue paper wrappers arrived in 1849 and sold for about a shilling per copy, *Nicholas Nickleby* in morocco binding with gilt edges and forty engravings was advertised by a Cape bookseller for fifteen shillings. It was in September of that year that *Sam Sly's African Journal* first serialised *David Copperfield* for wider readership, and sold more copies. Sly, whose real name was William Layton Sammons, had already reviewed *Martin Chuzzlewit* in an earlier issue. He had copied large extracts in the smallest possible type, probably because he had no legal right to do so.

Ironically, Sammons, who on occasion communicated with Dickens on literary matters, probably informed him in 1861 that the *Eastern Province Herald* in Port Elizabeth had reprinted chapters of *Great Expectations*. Dickens took prompt legal action to stop that newspaper from reprinting

---

[78] Quoted in Alan Hattersley (1973), p. 140. The full title of this novella is *The Chimes: A Goblin Story of Some Bells That Rang an Old Year Out and a New Year In*.

its original serialisation in his periodical *All the Year Round*.[79] The proprietors wrote a personal apology, and argued to no avail that their newspaper reached farmhouses where *All the Year Round* was unaffordable (Rochlin, 1957, p. 94). Reading had in fact become cheaper, but Dickens for the working classes did not sit well with some religious leaders and prudish readers. In his address to the subscribers of the South African Public Library in Cape Town in 1857, Reverend Henry White quoted Thomas Arnold who argued that 'exciting books of amusement like *Pickwick* and *Nickleby* . . . completely satisfy all the intellectual appetite of a boy . . . and leave him totally palled . . . for good literature'. Reverend White pointed out that Arnold had also listed *Oliver Twist* among the books that have 'increased the number of criminals and the depth of crimes' (Proceedings, 1857, pp. 13, 16).

And although Archdeacon Nathaniel Merriman, as chairman of the Grahamstown Public Library committee, welcomed working classes as 'evening readers' in the early 1860s, he viewed Dickens' novels as 'light works of merely passing amusement'. He took care that they 'should not be overabundant' (Hattersley, 1973, p. 245). In his 'Literary Reminiscences' presented to the Swellendam Literary Society in 1861, Reverend James Baker had, however, defended Dickens' realism in characterising the 'lower classes' as writing 'according to the age'. He quoted Richard Horne who in *A New Spirit of the Age* (1844) said of Dickens that he manages this so skilfully that his works may be read 'without a single offence to true and unaffected delicacy'.[80] But almost twenty years later, 'Two Moral Readers' still objected to having *Pickwick Papers* on the shelves of the Port Elizabeth Public Library. They complained to the editor of the *Eastern Province Herald* about its seduction and promotion of pugilism as evidence that 'a loose tone of morality pervades this author's writings' (Rochlin, 1957, p. 91).

More erudite criticism came from *The Cape of Good Hope Literary Magazine* editor. Commenting on *Dombey and Son* in 1847, James

---

[79] Cape Archives, CSC 2/6/1/40. *All the Year Round*, which incorporated *Household Words* in 1859, was available at some public libraries.

[80] Quoted in Baker, 1861, p. 98.

Fitzpatrick argued that Dickens' excellence, as in the case with *Pickwick*, is his caricatures or exaggeration of character. But when he tries to 'write like Scott, he fails as egregiously as Hogarth probably would have done had he striven to paint like Rembrandt'. In becoming popular, Fitzpatrick continued, he may have become 'too rapid in his execution – too anxious to produce surprises at the expense of sound literary propriety'.[81] It may ironically have been this exaggeration of character that strengthened Dickens' public appeal through entertainment. Beyond the literary reviews and sombre critique of his works there were 'stage adaptations and novel appropriations', although these may have delayed his recognition as a major and serious novelist (Humpherys, 2011, pp. 27–34). In England, adaptations of his novels included mime, music, dance, spectacle, and song. The English copyright law of 1842 did not prevent stage adaptations of novels, leaving Dickens and other authors helpless regarding their dramatisations both locally and abroad.

On the Podium

Popular interest in Dickens grew through formal lectures, and public readings of his works in urban and rural voluntary societies. At the Cape Town Mechanics Institute in December 1854, Professor Roderick Noble praised Dickens' writing in *Household Words* as 'in the very highest style of literary excellence'. His lecture, published in the *South African Commercial Advertiser*, recommended Dickens to the wider reading public (Rochlin, 1957, p. 89). At the same Institute a decade later, Mr. Advocate Cole's lecture – 'Some of the Humorous Writers of the Present Century' – included readings from Dickens' works, and were warmly praised by a newspaper correspondent.[82] In the Eastern Cape, the reputations of Dickens lecturers and readers were both celebrated and debated. A correspondent to the *Port Elizabeth Telegraph* in 1861, took issue with Bishop James Ricards' 'very interesting lecture' at a mutual improvement society for its criticism of Dickens' failure to show how to 'reclaim the

---

[81] *Cape of Good Hope Literary Magazine*, volume 2, pp. 449–50, 848.
[82] *Cape Argus*, 6 September, 1864.

unfortunate outcasts of society'.[83] The anonymous correspondent then quoted *Dombey and Son* as evidence to refute the Bishop's argument.

Journalist and newspaper owner Richard Murray (1894, p. 211), in his turn, explained that he preferred Bishop Ricards' reading of Charles Lever to that of Dickens, maintaining that he 'was never excelled in this country nor in any other'. In remote localities of the Colony of Natal in the 1860s, it was John Robinson who was the favourite Dickens lecturer and public reader. He recalled in his memoirs how listeners 'responded with laughter, or with tears, to the magic of his unmatched creations'.[84] Public response did not always reach these levels of critique and appreciation. At a mutual improvement society in the town of Colesberg, Mr Steytler's lecture in 1868 on 'Charles Dickens and his Writings' had a mixed reception. Perhaps it was the courtroom venue, borrowed for the occasion, which induced a few listeners to 'display their rough propensities by making a noise' (Rochlin, 1957, p. 90). Public readers sometimes suffered audiences' open displays of displeasure. The 'dramatist and reader' George Taylor Ferneyhough, who claimed also to be the manager of the Devonshire Dramatic and Elocution Club, was described in the *Cape Argus* as a mistake and 'not satisfactory to plebeians'. As a result, the greater number of those present walked out of the Mutual Hall room in Cape Town 'when the programme had yet a third of its course to run'.[85]

A *Standard and Mail* correspondent declared drily of Ferneyhough's reading that he 'gave a fashionable drawing room entertainment in the Mutual Hall last night and we seriously advise him not to give another'.[86] Inaccurate newspaper advertisements could have embarrassing results for public readers. The *Cape Argus* in July 1864 wrongly advertised a Mechanics Institute lecture by W. T. Hawthorne on William Thackeray instead of selected readings of his works. A letter of complaint from someone who attended was followed by outrage from Hawthorne and the secretary of the Mechanics Institute. The secretary suspected that the complainant was a member of the Catholic Young Men's Mutual Improvement Society,

[83] Bishop Ricards also delivered a lecture at the Graaff-Reinet Library in 1868.

[84] Christison (2012), p. 118. [85] *Cape Argus*, 10 July 1873.

[86] *Standard and Mail*, 8 July, 1873.

which also organised lectures for fund raising. He added that the Mechanics Institute often assisted them with chairs and rooms for such events.[87] Formal lectures and public readings of Dickens' works were, however, not as entertaining and appealing as their dramatisations for the stage, and it was *Pickwick Papers*, recited for the first time in Cape Town in 1851, that proved most popular.

On the Stage

Dramatisation made Dickens more popular and accessible across South Africa. But although prices were advertised as 'within reach of all classes of society', a separate entrance to the gallery for 'Coloureds' at a Cape Town theatre in 1860 confirms racial segregation (Bosman, 1980, p. 126). This did not deter 'non-White' audiences who even occupied the pit, and by 1875 a 'band of coloured boys picked from the streets of Cape Town' were on the stage for the first time (Fletcher, 1994, p. 99). In June 1860, the Amateur Theatrical Club of the small town of Richmond arranged and presented the *Trial of Bardell vs. Pickwick*.[88] Lines from the prologue, composed for this occasion, include the following:

> . . . Our desire to give dull times a fillip, and inspire
> Some genial warmth and mirth where both are *schaars*[89]
> Has brought us here to represent a farce . . .
> First then, tonight we'll put upon our stage
> What Dickens, in his laughter-moving page
> Has told of one fair widow who fell sick
> Of love for good old Samuel Pickwick . . .[90]

Pickwick featured prominently in town and countryside, as can be seen in a sample of dramatic readings and stage performances of Dickens in the 1860s, 1870s, and 1880s.[91]

---

[87] *Cape Argus*, 21 July, 28 July, and 1 August 1864.
[88] Richmond is regarded today as South Africa's 'book town'.
[89] Dutch for 'scarce'. [90] Rochlin, 1957, pp. 90–1.
[91] Extracted from newspapers, and Bosman (1980).

RICHMOND, 1860:	'Trial of Bardell vs Pickwick', *Pickwick Papers* – stage performance.
CAPE TOWN, 1861:	*The Cricket on the Hearth* – stage performance.
CAPE TOWN, 1864:	*David Copperfield* – dramatic reading.
WORCESTER, 1868:	'Mr Bumble and Mrs Corney', *Oliver Twist* – dramatic reading.
CAPE TOWN, 1868:	'The laughable trial of Bardell vs Pickwick', *Pickwick Papers* – stage performance.
CRADOCK, 1870:	'Mr Minns and his Cousin', *Sketches by Boz* – dramatic reading.
CAPE TOWN, 1871:	*Pickwick Papers* – dramatic reading.
CAPE TOWN, 1875:	'Little Emily', *David Copperfield* – stage performances on August 28th and 30th; September 1st, 18th ('last time'), and 27th ('positively last time'); 'My Child's Wife', *David Copperfield* – dramatic reading; 'Sam Weller's Valentine', *Pickwick Papers* – dramatic reading.
CAPE TOWN, 1876:	*Oliver Twist* – stage performance.
CAPE TOWN, 1883:	'Little Nell', *The Old Curiosity Shop*; 'Poor Little Jo', *Bleak House*; 'Little Emily', *David Copperfield* – stage performances.

Dramatic readings of *Pickwick Papers*, *Sketches by Boz*, and *Oliver Twist* were usually included in an 'Entertainment'. This was an occasion arranged in small towns, and advertised in local newspapers, usually to raise funds for their public libraries.[92] An 'Entertainment' was typically a variety concert consisting of two or more of the following: songs, instrumental recitals, dances, recitations, and minor dramas. They were fortnightly events during the winter months with admission for a small fee. Without professional entertainers, the programmes in these towns featured residents and members of local literary, musical, and scientific societies, as well as library

[92] *The Worcester Courant*, 18 September 1868; *The Queenstown Free Press*, 7 September and 9 November, 1859.

committee members. The Cradock 'Literary Entertainment' in April 1870 was reported in the local newspaper as the first of its kind in that town.[93] A special curtain of red, white, and blue was added to the stage of the hall used for the occasion. Mr R. W. Giddy read a 'selection from Dickens', and on the programme too were selections of music, a reading from *The Works of Douglas Jerold*, a song called '*The Wonderful Scholar*', and a reading of Charles Lever's '*The Adjutant's Story*'.

Perennial Pickwick

The popularity of *Pickwick Papers* would persist in the private reading and social life of Charlie Immelmann of Worcester,[94] where Penny Readings featured Dickens in the 1880s. Charlie's letter book and a commonplace book that he kept as a young man confirm *Pickwick* as a favourite. It was among the books he borrowed from the Worcester Public Library in 1885. The library committee had ordered it along with *Dombey and Son* from Juta's bookshop in Cape Town in October 1878.[95] Charlie wrote to a friend in 1888 requesting him to purchase copies of the sixpenny edition of *Pickwick*, as well as two copies of *Robinson Crusoe*. He intended to send them to some young women, and the choice of *Pickwick* for Kay de Vos may have been prompted by another of Charlie's correspondents who had recommended it as good preparation for married life and raising children.[96] Dickens, who Charlie calls 'my old friend', remained an enduring interest and he records in his diary for 1918 that *Oliver Twist* was one of the 'Bioscope Films' he saw that year.[97] Early appearances of Dickens on the screen in South Africa included *Edwin Drood* (1910), *Oliver Twist* (1910–11), *Little Em'ly* (1912), and *Pickwick Papers* (1913).[98]

---

[93] *Cradock and Tarkastad Register*, 22 April 1870.   [94] See Section 4.

[95] Minute Book, Public Library, Worcester, 1 October 1878.

[96] C. P. Immelman Collection, Stellenbosch University Library, Letter book entry for 8 August 1888.

[97] Diary for 1918, C.P. Immelman Collection.

[98] See Gutsche (1946), pp. 145, 170, 172, 174.

A more illustrious reader with *Pickwick* too in his private catalogue of books was Jan Hendrik Hofmeyr (Onze Jan).[99] As a young man in the 1860s, he was so familiar with *Pickwick* that he could recognise the character of Sam Weller in Dutch author Jacob van Lennep's *Ferdinand Huyck* (1840). He suspected that van Lennep had probably read *Pickwick* before producing this work (Hofmeyr & Reitz, 1913, p. 64). In 1869, *Pickwick* appears too among several of Dickens' titles in the catalogue of the St. Patrick's Catholic Young Men's Mutual Improvement Society in Grahamstown. It was here at about that time that Shakespeare-loving Robert Mullins listed *Pickwick* in his diary as one of the books he had read (Wright, 2008, p. 35). He had also read *Nicholas Nickleby* and *Dombey and Son*. So it was not just *Pickwick* that was singled out for mention in diaries and private letters as worth reading. In Durban in 1855, Marianne Churchill's diary records that she read *Bleak House*[100] before going on to read Thomas Macaulay's *Critical and Historical Essays* (Child, 1979, p. 63).

By the 1860s, Dickens seemed to be everywhere. His works were more accessible than those of other popular authors. Walter Scott was still a favourite, but Dickens' fiction in magazines was easier to find, and more readily available. In this way, Mrs. Moodie in Durban could, in 1863, read from his weekly periodical, *Master Humphrey's Clock*, to her friend Cary who was suffering from a boil on her foot (Rainier, 1974, p. 118). Innovative methods of publication and distribution strengthened Dickens' grip on the public imagination. His works could be read in the *Household Words* and *All the Year Round* periodicals that, along with his novels, were available at several public libraries. The 'Glimpses of Literature' columns in newspapers circulating in Aliwal North, Lady Grey, Dordrecht, and Basutoland featured *The Mystery of Edwin Drood* in 1870, and *The Light-hearted Traveler* in 1872.[101]

---

[99] J. H. Hofmeyr Papers, National Library of South Africa, MSC 8, 21 (1). Jan Hendrik Hofmeyr 'Onze Jan' was a well-known journalist and politician.

[100] This novel may have inspired Annie Clark, who was a member of the Ladies Pioneer Debating Club in Uitenhage, to name her residence *Bleak House* (Clark, 1897).

[101] *The Aliwal North Standard and Basutoland, Lady Grey and Dordrecht Register*, 31 December 1870; *The Aliwal Observer and Dordrecht and Lady Grey Times*,

Dickens' edited *Pic-Nic Papers* was included among the Railway Novels sold in Cape Town bookshops for two shillings each, and post-free for two shillings and nine pence.

Improvements to the railway network in the 1860s and 1870s sped up the transport of books from Cape Town publishers and booksellers to country-side bookshops, which advertised them in local newspapers. The Aliwal North Reading Club bought the *All the Year Round* periodical issues and Dickens' Christmas Books for its members. When it merged with the Aliwal North Public Library in 1873, more titles were added to the shelves (Aliwal North, 1903, p. 13). About 400 km away by road, the remote Barkly West Public Library, which listed twenty-one Dickens titles in its catalogue, included *Pickwick Papers* (Barkly West, 1886, p. 11). It was also listed in the catalogues of Kimberley Public Library and the Caledon Public Library, and several others across the countryside.

Dickens was read and discussed more widely and more often than authors with longer lists of titles. His novels, James Fairbairn had argued in a newspaper editorial in 1871, addressed the heart while Thackeray addressed the intellect. Fairbairn concluded that this was the reason why the majority of readers preferred him.[102] His works were then available too at auctions, and among the cheap reprints sold by the bookshops of J.C. Juta and W. Brittain. The name 'Pickwick' would remain popular and, intriguingly, in 1920, the Industrial and Commercial Workers Union announced that the Pickwick Cooperative Club in Cape Town had held an entertainment.[103]

The Pulpit and Political Stage

With improved accessibility and a wider readership, it was not unusual to find references to Dickens in private correspondence, as well as in public records, arguments, lectures, readings, debates, and even sermons. The liberal theologian, David Faure, advocated his works at Cape Town's Mutual Hall in a discourse about 'calling evil good' that was published in

8 June 1872. The newspaper probably renamed Dickens' *Uncommercial Traveller* in this way.

[102] *Cape Argus*, 7 October 1871.   [103] *The Black Man*, 1 (3), September 1920.

the *Standard & Mail* on 3 August 1878. On the harmful novels of the day that obscure 'the moral sense of many a one who reads them', Faure stated of Dickens that 'no man, no woman, and no child is not the better off for having read his books, books in which no single impure thought is to be found, no single corrupting sentence is to be met with'.[104] Faure, however, called evil good himself when he supported the controversial Contagious Diseases Act of 1885. Its main effect was to register prostitutes, and set a double standard that discriminated against women.

He instead asked 'mistaken purists' to recall Dickens' 'picture of true-hearted old Peggoty placing a candle in the window every evening as a beacon light to guide his loved and lost Em'ly when she perhaps would come home again' (Faure, 1907, p. 56). In the twentieth century, the moral, literary, and entertainment references to Dickens' works would increasingly give way to their political applications in South Africa's liberation struggle. Richard Godlo, arguing for the rights denied to Africans, quoted on more than one occasion in the 1920s from *The Chimes*: 'But gentlemen, gentlemen, dealing with other men like me begin at the right end ... Give us kinder laws to bring us back when we're a-going wrong; and don't set jail, jail, jail afore us, everywhere we turn' (Davenport, 1973, p. 10). In the 1950s, Jack Cope argued that Dickens was 'a man of the people, and a dyed-in-the-wool radical'.[105] And his later novels, where 'the gap between wealth and poverty was most painfully described', inspired Jean Middleton to become a communist.[106]

Es'kia Mphahlele staged scenes from *A Tale of Two Cities* in Johannesburg townships because of the 'relevance of protest against an oppressive regime', and because Dickens was more direct than Shakespeare (Peterson, 1989, p. 32). In 1963, Pip's attempt to help Abel Magwitch escape from the authorities in *Great Expectations* saved political activist Ronnie Kasrils from arrest by security police (Kasrils, 1998, pp. 57–8). By candlelight and moonlight, in the 1970s, student activists read his works in Soweto and other townships as 'allies' in the liberation struggle. And in 1987, *Great*

---

[104] Calling Evil Good. *Standard & Mail*, 3 August 1878.
[105] Charles Dickens, the Radical. *Guardian*, 20 July 1950, p. 4.
[106] Middleton, *Convictions*, p. 42.

Expectations was, perhaps for optimistic reasons, in constant circulation at the B Section library of Pollsmoor Maximum Prison that housed Nelson Mandela and some of his comrades.[107] Mandela's comrade and prison librarian Ahmed Kathrada also listed the 113-minute long film version of *Great Expectations* for viewing in that year.

Conclusion

In the spaces of literary improvement and entertainment in the nineteenth century, communities read, heard, lent, borrowed, performed, quoted, copied, critiqued, gifted, repurposed, preached, and screened Dickens' works. These would become spaces of protest and revolution across anti-apartheid organisations in the twentieth century. His early humoristic works, and the later works in which social criticism featured more prominently, assured Dickens' reputation in South Africa.[108] They had endeared him to Charlie Immelman whose admiration crossed over from reading his novels to viewing their screen adaptations in small town cinemas. The rapidly increasing number of subscription 'public' libraries made Dickens' works, and those of some of the world's best and most popular writers, more widely accessible to ordinary readers and cinema patrons like Charlie.

4 The Fiction Charlie Immelman Read, and the Films He Watched

'I spend nearly every day in the Public Library here', Charlie Immelman (1870–1937) wrote in his diary on Friday, 20 June 1890, in Worcester. Established in 1854 and accommodated initially in a Town Hall room, Worcester Public Library was among the Cape Colony's seventy government-supported public libraries by 1890.[109] Any interested groups of people

---

[107] Ahmed Kathrada Collection, Mayibuye Archives, Bellville, File 13.1 and File 13.4. Also listed in the Unity Movement's South Peninsula Educational Fellowship library catalogue.

[108] His death in 1870 was announced alongside reviews in the Cape and country newspapers.

[109] *Cape of Good Hope Blue Book. Reports of Public Libraries for 1890*, p. 22.

in 'smaller towns' that had collected subscriptions and donations to the value of £25 for the first or average of two years could register for an annual grant.[110] Countryside book, reading, and other voluntary societies, like those in Aliwal-North, Bredasdorp, Colesberg, Paarl, and Wodehouse quickly took up this offer.[111] As a condition of the grant, Worcester's library was open for reading and reference to the public free of charge from 9am to 8pm in summer, and 9am to 7pm in winter. Its Annual Report for 1885 reveals that members of the public had made 454 'visits' in that year.[112] The grant was a generous concession to the Worcester reading community whose population figure (urban and rural) stood at 12,615 in 1891. Of its 5,539 persons able to read and write, 3,772 (68 per cent) were 'Whites', and 1,767 (32 per cent) were 'Other than European or Whites' (Results of a Census, 1892, p. 214).[113]

Charlie was one of thirty-eight members[114] who, for an annual fee of £1.00, also had access to the subscribers' room in the library where the latest newspapers were kept, and he could borrow books and magazines. As a sixteen-year-old in 1886, Charlie described himself as 'a body on two legs, 5 ft 3in high in a suit of blue serge, short trousers, brown stockings, straw hat, black boots, no beard, dog eyes and large red nose, in all a rascally young boer' (Schaafsma, 2005, p. 3). This was just a year after he started listing the books and their authors, in the order that he had read them, for each year that he lived or worked in several small towns. The first lists are for 1885 to 1887, and appear at the end of his letter books that served also as diaries, and into which he copied the letters he wrote to and received from friends. A book list appears again in 1890 in a standard-type diary, and

---

[110] *Memorandum of Regulations to Encourage Public Libraries in Smaller Towns of the Colony*, 28 May 1874.

[111] *Replies to Circular, 1873–4, CO 4692*, Cape Archives.

[112] *Worcester Weekly News*, 21 January 1886.

[113] The figures for the Cape Colony's population of 1,527,224 in 1891 were 75.34 per cent and 24.66 per cent respectively for those able to read and write.

[114] There were eighty members by 1905. *Minute Book, Public Library, Feb 1895 – Feb 1921*, Worcester Public Library.

then they continue from 1906 to 1927 with just a few years omitted.[115] They reveal over 280 titles, primarily works of fiction that he also started rating with an 'x' (or star) from about 1917 – 'xxxx' (four stars) being the highest rating. He also kept a separate commonplace book with favourite passages copied from some of these works. From August 1919 to 1922, he listed the titles and main actresses in the seventy 'bioscope films' that he saw, many of which he rated in the same way. This intriguing record of books and films offers an insight into the mind and imagination of a middle-class reader who lived in several of the Cape's small towns during a period of significant events in its history.

Libraries and books featured prominently in the Immelman family. Carl Lindenberg, Charlie's grandfather on his mother's side, was the first librarian of the Stellenbosch subscription library in 1859.[116] Charlie's father, Stephanus Immelman, was a member of the Worcester Public Library committee in the early 1870s. His brother S. A. Immelman helped to start a public library in Britstown in 1893 (Immelman, 1970, p. 76). And his nephew, R. F. M. Immelman, was a respected scholar and the university librarian at the University of Cape Town from 1940 to 1970. Charlie was one of eight children and lived next to the family's chemist and shop. His middle-class childhood afforded him 'productive leisure time' to nurture the skills he would need as an adult. As Duff (2011, p. 500) explains, 'he corresponded with a wide circle of friends and relatives scattered around the Boland and Cape Town; went swimming in summer; edited a spoof newspaper called the *Worcester Knobkirrie*; attended the sittings of the circuit court with some enthusiasm; paid to see travelling circuses and minstrels; and collected stamps'. He attended the Worcester Boys Public School, and after passing the Civil Service examination in December 1890, he started working for an attorney.

---

[115] Ms 321, C.P. Immelman documents, in P. W. Immelman collection, Manuscript Section, Stellenbosch University Library. Earlier diaries not found in this collection may also have included books.

[116] Thanks to Anneke Schaafsma for several pieces of information used in this Section.

Following a courtship of about eight years and a correspondence of more than 700 letters, he married Joey Retief in March 1899 (Schaafsma, 2005, p. 7). They had one child, Stephanus Rhyno, who became an architect. Charlie wrote in English, but, like everyone in Worcester, he spoke Dutch. He was sworn in as a Dutch interpreter in 1893, and appointed as a clerk in the Department of the Master of the Supreme Court in Cape Town. In 1912, he became an Assistant Resident Magistrate in Caledon and, by 1918, he was the Resident Magistrate at Indwe. His career involved transfers to several small towns, in the following order, with the year when their public libraries were established: Grahamstown (1863), Kimberley (1882), Beaconsfield (1889), Paarl (1872), Beaufort-West (1857), Fraserburg (1866), Van Rhynsdorp (1950), Uitenhage (1858), Paarl again, Caledon (1886), Malmesbury (1858), Indwe (1896), Wellington (1879), Middelburg (1878), Piketberg (1872), and Somerset-East (1869).[117] He and Joey settled in Paarl after his retirement in the early 1930s.[118] All of these towns, except Van Rhynsdorp and Indwe, already had public libraries by the time his travels started in the early 1890s. Detailed financial records in his diaries list library subscription payments to some of them. They confirm that, in 1920, he was a member of Wellington Public Library and, by 1926, a year before the lists end, he was a member of Piketberg Public Library. They show also that he purchased books and newspapers and subscribed to magazines, which he moved with his other possessions from town to town.

Reading fiction

In his mid-twenties, his magazine subscriptions included *Answers* and *Home Chat*, and by March 1918, then married and middle-aged, there were payments for the *American Journal* and *Homestead*.[119] He bought some of his books and magazines at the sales arranged by public library committees to raise funds. The Worcester Public Library regularly sold its old newspapers and magazines, although some like *The Graphic* and *Illustrated*

---

[117] During the South African War (1899–1902) Charlie lived in Van Rhynsdorp, and in 1918, during the Spanish flu epidemic, he was in Indwe.

[118] He passed away on 29 June 1937.

[119] Expenses in diary entries for April 1895 and March 1918.

London News were presented to Worcester's 'Deaf and Dumb Institute'.[120] At the end of just his third list as a teenager, Charlie adds that he had also read 'some volumes of *Boy's Own Paper*, *Sunday at Home*, *Chambers' Journal*, etc, etc.' Many public libraries subscribed to these magazines, and those, like *Chambers' Journal*, included fiction that were popular too with working class visitors. When the Queenstown Public Library (est. 1859), for example, opened its non-subscribers reading room containing several newspapers and magazines freely to the public, Van der Walt (1972, p. 61) reports that crowds of 'coloured readers' turned up merely to 'look at the pictures'.

This is not entirely correct because the census of 1865 states that in Queenstown, where 2,180 'Whites' could read and write, 578 'Blacks and those of mixed descent' could also read.[121] They would have taken advantage of that library's grant-based concession because most could not afford the subscription fee, and because racial discrimination by several library committees remained rife into the early twentieth century. Whereas the Port Elizabeth Library committee secretary acknowledged that 'coloured people . . . cannot be lawfully excluded', the East London Library committee chairman said 'we do not allow them nor do we intend to do so in future'. The Kimberley Library committee refused the subscription from 'a local Non-White', and returned his fee to him (Peters, 1974, p. 25). At several public libraries many non-subscribers, as in Queenstown, could and did, however, use the public reading room. They were calculated into the official statistics recorded for daily visitors at all the public libraries across the Cape Colony. The number reached 4,360 per day by 1909,[122] although the true figure must have been higher because not everyone signed the library's 'Daily Attendance Register'.

Like 'White' library visitors, they too would have read the serialised and illustrated fiction available in *Blackwoods*, *Harpers*, *Cornhill*, *Murray's*, and *Macmillan's magazines*, to which many public libraries subscribed. At Port Elizabeth Public Library in 1861, *Macmillan's Magazine* was identified with

---

[120] *Minute Book, Worcester Public Library*, 27 October 1902.

[121] *Census of the Colony of the Cape of Good Hope*, 1865, p. 63.

[122] *Cape of Good Hope Blue Book. Reports of Public Libraries for 1909*, p. 188.

Tom Brown's School Days, described as 'a delightful Tale which everybody is reading'.[123] And not just in the Cape Colony, because even as far away as Melbourne in Australia seventeen-year-old Joyce Sincock had just read *Tom Brown* in the same April 1861 issue of *MacMillan's Magazine* (Martin, 2014, p. 41). And this would be the second title, twenty-five years later, in sixteen-year-old Charlie's book list in Worcester, but it was the book version by Thomas Hughes – or in Charlie's abbreviation of the original author description – by 'An old boy'. When Charlie started his book lists in 1885, fiction accounted for well above 60 per cent of the total number of items circulated at Worcester Public Library. For the period 1910 to 1930, when his book lists had ended, the average annual figure was 63.7 per cent.

In his first book list, the sea stories of Frederick Marryat and juvenile fiction of Robert Ballantyne feature alongside Mark Twain's *Adventures of Huckleberry Finn* and Walter Scott's *Kenilworth*. As a teenager and 'rascally young boer', one wonders whether and how Charlie compared British author Mary Ann Carey-Hobson's realist novel, *The Farm in the Karoo*, with his own observations of rural Worcester. In the lists for 1886 and 1887, there are adventure, romantic, and detective mystery novels, although room is made for Edwin Paxton Hood's *The World of Anecdote*. Dramatic changes in South Africa because of the recent discovery of gold may have influenced his choice of the Belgian Hendrik Conscience's Dutch-language *Het Goudland*, a novel about the California gold rush. If observations of current events and personal experiences indeed played a role in his reading choices, then Charlie's regular visits to Worcester's circuit court as a teenager may have influenced his selection in 1886 of James Redding Ware's *Before the Bench*: *Sketches of Police Court Life*. This book in some ways too presaged his career as a travelling court clerk and later as a magistrate. H. Rider Haggard, whose *King Solomon's Mines* he read in 1890, would later feature also as a favourite author.

The book lists resume in 1906 when Charlie is an adult, married, a father, and no longer living in Worcester.[124] They are shorter, indicating that he may have had less time for reading as he adapted to work pressures and

---

[123] Our Library Table, *Eastern Province Magazine*, 1, 1861, p. 32.
[124] It is uncertain whether diaries for the intervening years are missing.

family responsibilities. Hall Caine's *The Christian*, which is said to have been the first novel in Britain to sell one million copies, and which was subsequently produced as a silent movie, heads the list.[125] Fergus Hume's *Hagar of the Pawnshop: The Gypsy Detective*, *The Veiled Man* by William Le Queux, and Walter Besant's *For Faith and Freedom* confirm that his interest in detective mysteries, adventure, and romantic fiction had not waned. These authors and titles were popular, and they were listed in the catalogues of the rural Aliwal North and Barkly West Public Libraries, as well as that of Kimberley Public Library where Charlie was a subscriber while he worked in that town.[126] Charlie's sustained interest in romantic fiction may have had something to do with his 'eye for a pretty girl', and 'at least three relationships with girls in Worcester'.[127] In a letter copied into his diary in 1887, one young woman promised to let him have her copy of Annie Swan's *Mark Desborough's Vow*, which she had read through three times. Charlie's diary reveals too that he bought some books for girls he knew, and when he started courting Joey he read aloud to her 'under shady trees'.[128]

His familiarity with romantic fiction writers worked in his favour. A letter in January 1892 addressed Joey as 'My dear Little Mystery', and promised that if she would see him that weekend he would bring along Augusta Evans Wilson's *Infelice*. Her affirmative reply concluded with 'Little Mystery ends', and in a subsequent letter she described other books that he had loaned her as 'indeed splendid'. But she was hesitant to pass them on to her Aunt in Wellington who also wanted to read them. The reason, she explained, is Charlie's 'marks and writing' in them, which must

---

[125] Waller, P. (2006). *Writers, Readers, and Reputations: Literary Life in Britain 1870–1918*. Oxford University Press, p.731.

[126] Aliwal North Public Library. Catalogue of Books (1903). Northern Post and Border News; Barkly West Public Library and Reading Room. Catalogue of Books (n.d.). Grocott & Sherry; Alphabetical List of the Kimberley Public Library (1884). Radford and Roper.

[127] Schaafsma, p. 7; Duff, p. 500.

[128] Ms 321, C.P. Immelman documents, Diary for May 22nd, 1887 to August 28th, 1888, columns 741–3; Notebook for 1 January to 29 March 1891.

have been too intimate for a close relative to read.[129] Augusta Evans Wilson's sentimental novels had become Cupid's arrows in Charlie's arsenal. This is why he promised Joey other works by Wilson from his own 'little library which is getting stocked nicely month by month'.[130] And the large number of romantic novels in his book lists, following their marriage in 1899, confirms that he continued to share these books with her. As a member of several libraries, he may well have borrowed romantic novels for both himself and Joey to read and discuss. Popular authors in his lists included Annabella B. Marchand, Elinor Glyn, Florence L. Barclay, and Ethel M. Dell.

Marie Corelli's *The Treasure of Heaven* and Hall Caine's *The Prodigal Son* were bestsellers in England and South Africa in the first decade of the twentieth century (Forrest, 1907, p. 69). They are not in Charlie's lists, but he read Caine's *The Eternal City* in 1911, and he would read Corelli's *Wormwood* in 1927. Books by other favourite authors that he listed at this time were Baroness Orczy's *The Scarlet Pimpernel*, *The Elusive Pimpernel*, and *Petticoat Government*, as well as H. Rider Haggard's *Lysbeth*, and *The Ivory Child*. Haggard's popularity in South Africa was then on the wane, although *Jess* was still considered a classic. Olive Schreiner's *The Story of an African Farm* was also widely read and appreciated, but according to one commentator this was more for its subtle 'atmosphere' than as a piece of literature (Forrest, 1907, p. 72). Other contemporary novelists that focused on South Africa included Ernest Glanville, Bertram Mitford, and Douglas Blackburn. Their works were available in several public libraries, but they are not in Charlie's lists. The reasons, as Forrest (1907, p. 73) explained, may have been the deluge of general fiction during the English publishing seasons, and because of the failure of South African newspaper editors to publicise the work of emerging local writers like Glanville.

Charlie's novel-rating system did not connect in a straightforward way with his commonplace book, making it difficult to establish who his most-

---

[129] Ms 321, Letter from Joey Retief to Charlie Immelman, 30 April 1892.

[130] This letter lists Wilson's *St Elmo*, *Beulah*, *At the Mercy of Tiberius*, *Inez*, *Macaria*, and *Vashti*. Ms 321, Letter from Charlie Immelman to Joey Retief, 16 September 1892. These and other books may be listed in diaries for the missing years, 1888–1905.

favoured novelists were, and why. In 1918 he assigned three stars to Broadway's novel about the Transvaal, *The Longest Way Round*, and he copied several passages from it into his commonplace book. But although he also copies passages from Rosa Carey's *The Key of the Unknown*, this novel receives no rating. Similarly, Herbert Jenkins' *The Night Club* receives no rating, but there are several passages from it in his commonplace book. And J. M Barrrie's *The Little Minister* gets a two-star rating, as well as copied passages in his commonplace book. It is unclear therefore what criteria he used to rate these novels, but the commonplace book passages seem to have been selected for their eloquence and turns of phrase. He may have considered them useful for professional or personal reasons.

Reading Fiction and Watching Films

Charlie's reading lists during the First World War reveal the usual mix of adventure, mystery, and romance novels. But in 1919, he read Sapper's (Herman McNeile) war novel *No Man's Land* (unrated). He also read *The Dop Doctor* (one-star rating) by Richard Dehan (Clotilde Graves), the film version of which was considered offensive in South Africa because of the portrayal of Dutch Afrikaner ('Boer') character. It had been banned in the United Kingdom in 1914, and its prohibition from being shown in South Africa in 1916 precipitated the enactment of film censorship legislation (Gutsche, 1946, pp. 395–8). Negative portrayals of White women and men more generally, regarded as the 'loss of European prestige', also influenced censors' decisions on what films Black South Africans were allowed to see (Paleker, 2014, p. 316). Whether Charlie eventually saw *The Dop Doctor* is uncertain, but from 15 August 1919 he started adding, alongside the books, lists of the silent films that he saw and rated as well. Visits to the cinema had already started a few years earlier, and his record of expenses for January 1916 shows that he spent nine shillings for that purpose. Joey usually accompanied him to the cinema. Shared entertainment began during their courtship when Charlie first promised to take her to see the pantomime *Beauty and the Beast* in Cape Town.[131]

---

[131] Ms 321, Letter from Charlie Immelman to Joey Retief, 16 September 1892.

Whereas the books he read generally provided 'improvement', the films instead supplied 'entertainment'. His expense records show considerable sums of money spent on them every year. 'Bioscope films', as Charlie and other South Africans called them, were first screened at the Empire Variety Theatre in Johannesburg in 1896, and soon thereafter in Cape Town bioscopes. 'Talkies' only arrived in 1929, so that what he and Joey saw in 1919 were silent films, which had 'intertitles' or text that could be read across the filmed action on the screen. The bioscope had in effect become another 'reading space' for text and image. Since 1909, private companies brought travelling or 'touring cinemas' to small towns or 'dorps'. By the 1920s, permanent bioscopes in the Cape countryside included 'Grabouw Kinema' (Elgin), 'Elite Kinema' (Paarl), 'Astoria Kinema' (Queenstown), and 'Pavilion Kinema' (Strand). And there was one under construction in Worcester (Gutsche, 1946, p. 283). When Charlie and Joey were living in Indwe in 1919, they visited the bioscope monthly. Two of the films they saw – *Thelma* and *Rags* – were regarded as outstanding films for that year in South Africa (Gutsche, 1946, p. 268).

Macbeth was also considered outstanding in 1919, but it is not on Charlie's list. Instead he assigned three stars to the American drama films *Battle of Hearts* and *The Eleventh Commandment*. On the list also are films based on books such as Charles Kingsley's historical novel *Westward Ho*, Charles Dickens' *Oliver Twist*, and Rex Beach's Western *Heart of the Sunset*. Fiction films were an important development in the first decades of the twentieth century. This resulted in longer films that introduced 'stars' or main actresses, and Charlie routinely added their names to his lists from 1920 onwards. He was the Resident Magistrate in Wellington in that year, and frequented the movies more often. His expense record for the 'bioscope' in December alone reveals five visits either by himself, or with Joey and other friends. The list of thirty silent films for 1920 ranges across adventure, romance, and mystery. The First World War is the background for the melodrama *Fields of Honour* (three stars), as well as *Service Star* (three stars) that features the actress Madge Kennedy. She stars too in *Through the Wrong Door* and *Day Dreams* that they saw that year.

He and Joey may have especially admired the film actresses whose names recur on several lists. Madge Kennedy, for example, was a stage, film, and television actress who was also involved in radio and film production. Another favourite actress, Lilian Walker, set up her own production company in 1918 and produced *The Embarrassment of Riches*. And Mary Pickford, who was on almost all of the film lists as well as Gutsche's annual lists of outstanding films in South Africa, was a successful businesswoman who started an organisation to help financially needy actors. He (and Joey?) gave the highest film rating (four stars) to the murder mystery *Vanity*. This is itself something of a mystery since it does not feature on any of Gutsche's annual lists of outstanding films screened in South Africa. Mysteriously too Emily Wehlen, the main actress, vanished from the public eye while in her early thirties.[132]

Equally intriguing is whether Charlie saw the 1926 film based on Bithia Mary (B. M.) Croker's book, *The Road to Mandalay*, which he had read in 1918. Croker and Fanny Emily (F. E.) Penny, whose book *A Question of Colour* Charlie read in 1927, were British women who wrote Anglo-Indian romances. Both used their initials only when they started writing, probably because of the themes of their novels. As in *A Question of Colour*, interracial relationships feature again in Penny's *A Mixed Marriage*. Did contemporary race relations in South Africa influence Charlie's reading choices? Or, if at all, did the reading of novels about racial identity and cultural mixing enter into his thoughts and judgements as a small-town magistrate? It may not be coincidental that he read *A Question of Colour* in the same year (1927) that South Africa's Immorality Act, which forbade sexual intercourse between Africans and Europeans, was passed.

Some novels, like A. M. S Hutchinson's *If Winter Comes*, which he read in 1922, became a silent film in 1923 as well as a play, but there is no indication that he saw either. Fiction films were also made locally, and it may be possible that Charlie saw Rider Haggard's *Allan Quatermain* that was produced by African Film Productions, and shown throughout the Union in 1919 (Gutsche, 1946, p. 432). He describes the three films in his final list in 1922 as 'Good Bioscope Films', suggesting that not all that he had seen that year were worth listing. This may explain why, in spite of an expense item in his diary for money spent on the 'bioscope' in May 1926, no

---

[132] None of Charlie's books have a four-star rating.

titles are listed for that year. By that time, between three and five films were typically screened in a single bioscope show. One may only speculate whether he and Joey saw the silent films based on novels by Rafael Sabatini and Peter Kyne that he read in 1925. He had continued to subscribe to the public libraries in the small towns where he worked and, although they were no longer rated, he read more books with a local flavour.

Charlie may purposefully have sought out and read novels written by fellow members of South Africa's legal profession, such as magistrate W. C. Scully's *The Harrow* and attorney L. H. Brinkman's *The Glory of the Backveld*. As a civil servant of the British government at the Cape during the South African War (1899–1902), Charlie had to comply with instructions. In 1910, he had, however, read J. L. De Villiers' *Hoe Ik Ontsnapte*, an account of an Afrikaner's escape from a British concentration camp in India. It is unclear whether or not he had interpreted this book more as travel literature than war writing, as the literary scholar Nienke Boer (2017) does. But his reading of *The Harrow*, which is fictional but based on cases of war crimes committed by the British forces in the Transvaal and Orange Free State republics, must have been more unsettling.[133] He records in his diary for 1901 that a Boer commando entered Van Rhynsdorp where he was living at the time, and that the British occupied it following skirmishes just outside the town (Schaafsma, 2005, p. 8).

Some of the books in his last few lists have a higher literary value. In 1925, he read Joseph Conrad's *The Secret Agent*, a political novel and satire of English society. There is also *Arrowsmith*, for which Sinclair Lewis was awarded the Pulitzer Prize in 1926 (which he declined). In his final list is John Galsworthy's *Caravan*, which won the Nobel Prize for Literature in 1932. His reading taste had now diversified to include Stephen Leacock's *Nonsense Novels* and Richard Dehan's *Earth to Earth* in the early 1920s, as well as Marie Corelli's modernist novel *Wormwood*, considered to be avant-garde writing of the period.[134]

---

[133] Scully's novel was based on the cases investigated by a commission that he chaired after the war.

[134] Modernist Mental States and Marie Corelli's Wormwood. www.ncgsjournal .com/issue42/shaffer.htm. Accessed 23 December 2019.

Conclusion

Charlie's sustained reading record is due in no small way to well-run public libraries in the fifteen small towns where he lived and worked. Before the era of professional librarians, the selection of materials was the job of volunteers who were often also library committee members, or 'friends' of the library. The efforts of some like C. Louis Leipoldt, M. E. Rothmann, and Francis Carey Slater who became prominent literary figures, contributed to developing the literary tastes of subscribers and 'visitors' who could not afford the subscription fee. Together they used public libraries to cultivate a unique ethos of improvement in the long nineteenth century. For the country's small religious communities, however, improvement required resources and services in languages such as Arabic, Malayu, Urdu, Gujarati, Tamil, Yiddish, and others. In the case of the Cape Muslim reading community, its distinctive literacy and literary practices forged connections with global Islamic printing networks.

5 The Cape's Global Islamic Printing Networks

In the second half of the nineteenth century, Cape Muslim scholars and entrepreneurs forged links with global Islamic printing networks. This triggered another transnational movement of people, technology, languages, and pan-Islamic ideas.[135] It also improved literacy, and nurtured reading and writing cultures in a small religious community in South Africa. Between 1822 and 1891, the number of Muslims in Cape Town grew from 3,000 to 11,287. And throughout the twentieth century, Muslims remained a minority in the country and did not rise to much more than 2 per cent of the population (Haron, 2013; Tayob, 1995, p. 45). This community derived its initial origins primarily from the Malaysian Peninsula and archipelago, as well as other parts of the Indian Ocean basin. As a result, there were languages other than just *Malayu*, and, after 1838, Dutch-Afrikaans in the Arabic script became the dominant language for written communication.

Throughout the Dutch East India Company (VOC) period of rule, Muslims from its possessions were among those brought as slaves to Cape

---

[135] Muslims arrived at the Cape since the mid seventeenth century.

Town, or banished as political exiles to Robben Island (Shell, 2000).
Muslims continued to arrive under British rule, and, from the 1860s, the
immigration of indentured labourers included Tamil-speaking Muslims
brought to Durban from India. Gujarati and Urdu-speaking Muslims,
many of whom were traders and merchants, followed the indentured
labourers to service this market. As business competitors, they faced
prohibitive legislation and stiff resentment from Durban's White settler
community. Then there were the so-called 'Zanzibaris', the majority of
whom were Muslims. They were actually liberated slaves brought as
indentured labourers to Durban from Northern Mozambique in the 1870s
and 1880s, and spoke Makua and Swahili (Kaarsholm, 2014).

These language groups' secondary migration to Cape Town in the late
nineteenth and early twentieth centuries added to the diversity of its Muslim
community. Then Kokani-speaking Indians from the Bombay Presidency
arrived and were soon followed by family members in the 1960s. Their
marriage into the Muslim community gave Cape Islam an even more
distinctive religious and cultural character (Tayob, 1995, pp. 54–8). There
were also African, English, Scottish, and Welsh converts that resulted from
Islamic proselytisation or *da'wah* (Rhoda, 2007). It is not surprising that, in
1925, the Christian missionary Samuel Zwemer, known as the 'apostle of
Islam', came across printed books for sale in Arabic-Afrikaans, Arabic-
Urdu, and Arabic-Gujarati in Cape Town's Muslim quarter (Zwemer, 1925,
p. 349). He reported that Cape Muslims spoke in English, Dutch, Afrikaans,
Urdu, Gujarati, Tamil, and Malay.[136]

Zwemer also found an Islamic catechism in English that had been printed
in Cape Town in 1914, and another in Dutch-Afrikaans printed by Breda
Printing Works in Noorder-Paarl. These publications were sold at little
bookshops that also stocked books printed in Arabic and Persian (Farsi).
Zwemer (1925, p. 349) speculated that 'a larger percentage of the people are
literate than perhaps in any other section of the Moslem world'. The
bookshops in Cape Town's Muslim quarter were run as family businesses,
and signified a growing demand for printed reading material in a vibrant
religious market. Robert Darnton's (1982) communications circuit connects

---

[136] For the use of Arabic-Malay (jawi) by the Cape Muslims, see Jappie (2012).

writers, publishers, printers, bookshops, libraries, and readers: In the case of this small Muslim community at the tip of Africa it would need to add *madrasahs* (Muslim schools) and mosques. They provided religious and secular education for this community's integration into the Cape's globalising economy.

Zwemer did not know that literacy among the Cape Muslims had developed over a long period, nor that its printing networks extended to the major Islamic cities of Constantinople (Istanbul), Bombay, Cairo, as well as the Anjouan and Zanzibar islands. As in early modern Europe, the growth of literacy in the early Cape's Islamic community was measured according to sign-literacy, or the ability to sign one's name (Biewenga, 1996, pp. 110–11). Signatures were typically found in official documents such as contracts, wills, and marriage registers. This prevented an accurate quantification of sign-literacy among the majority of Muslims because of their socio-economic status as slaves, and because they were not allowed to marry until 1823 (Mountain, 2004, p. 40). There is, however, ample evidence of the signatures of Muslim slaves and Free Blacks both in Roman letters and Arabic letters (Harris, 1977, pp. 170–1). And although many signed their wills with crosses, 'the ability to read and write in Arabic script was widespread' because reading the *Koran* in Arabic was important for Cape Muslim slaves (Davids, 1990, p. 17).

Print literacy was not only transplanted into the African context. It was translated, interpreted, recontextualised, and re-embedded by local people. New Literacy Studies, which emphasises 'situated literacies', offer a fuller understanding of early Cape Muslim literacy (Prinsloo & Baynham, 2008). Reading and writing in these approaches are rooted in conceptions of knowledge, identity, and being. Bickford-Smith (2003) affirms a connection between early printed publications, such as newspapers and books, and the fashioning of South Africa's racial or ethnic identities. This is evident too in the production of *koplesboeke* (student notebooks), Arabic-Afrikaans or *ajami* manuscripts, and printed 'Malay books' that were integral to the Cape Islamic religious identity. To these 'publications', one may add the literacy practices of chanting, memorising, reciting, reading aloud in groups, using texts as amulets, copying manuscripts, and circulating tracts, as well as subsequent printing practices (Haron, 2006).

Cape Muslims since the late eighteenth century propagated an alternative education to construct their independent identity. A system of *madrasahs*, mosques, *Imams* (Muslim priests), and teachers sought to eradicate illiteracy, and to empower slaves and Free Blacks (Shell, 2006). The *madrasah*-mosque complex of literacy agencies laid the foundations of a book and reading culture through the copying and circulating of manuscripts. By the mid nineteenth century, the potential for writing and the desire for reading made printing a necessity, and the first product at the Cape was a printed book in Arabic lettering in 1856 (Willemse & Dangor, 2011, pp. 84–5). Closer analysis of connections with African and global Islamic printing networks reveals distinctive features of the Cape Muslim community's identity, as well as its reading and writing cultures. Whereas the VOC established printing presses and used Malay printing types in Batavia and its other possessions since the second half of the seventeenth century, the Cape of Good Hope was an exception. On the other hand, the VOC had no clearly spelled-out book policy.

As a result, an 'ocean of books', often hidden between clothes in the trunks of sailors, circulated via ships' holds and were bartered in ports like Cape Town (Delmas, 2014, p. 213). These may well have included printed books in Arabic, Malay, and other Islamic languages, and come from other parts of Africa. There is a growing recognition that writing and printing, and therefore the history of the book in Africa, did not start with the arrival of the Latin script and of European missionary presses. One of the reasons why we know so little about this is that bodies of scholarship about these matters are separated from each other, and listed under different search headings (Jeppie, 2014, pp. 94–104). Sources on the material aspects of the making of texts, and on texts as objects, that should be related are actually separated from each other. Also, Arabic script by Muslim scholars is found under 'Islam in Africa', and Latin script by mission-educated elites is found under 'Intellectual history'. But new research tools are bringing these bodies of scholarship into conversation with each other. This will throw light on the complex circumstances in which the Cape's and other African Islamic communities' reading, writing, copying, and printing practices actually developed.

These tools may also generate the empirical evidence to better understand *Al Nahda*, or the literary-cultural awakening, in Egypt and other Arabic-speaking countries in the Middle East in the late nineteenth and early twentieth centuries (Ayalon, 2008, 2010). And this evidence could elaborate Nile Green's 'Islamic religious economy' about multiple interactions in the production of newspapers, travelogues, hagiographies, etiquette books, *et cetera*, in religious markets across the Indian Ocean, even as far south as Durban (Green, 2011, p. 218). His 'religious economy' idea shows how, when, and where global Islamic printing networks and markets emerged and expanded. It explains aspects of the Cape's Islamic printing networks especially with Bombay, but like *Al Nahda* it is not enough to explain this community's multiple connections over a longer period and across a wider geographical area. The distinctive features of the Cape Muslim community's reading, writing, and copying practices, and how they actually worked, more fully explain the development of local printing networks and how, when, and why they connected with global printing networks.

The first feature is that religious and economic rivalry spurred the production and distribution of reading materials in the Cape's Christian and Islamic communities, becoming more intense in the late eighteenth century. But before and after the Cape's printing era commenced in 1784, and in order to propagate their views, Christian and Islamic pietist priests encouraged readers to reproduce religious materials through a copying process. The paper that Christian and Muslim readers used to produce these copies was often sourced from the same European papermakers. The Dutch *Pro Patria* watermark, for example, appears on the paper used to produce both the 'Muslim' Johardien family's manuscripts in 1806, as well as the 'Christian' Ballot family's booklets from 1794 to 1810 (Dick, 2015, pp. 30–1). In both families, their homes were treasured spaces for reading these manuscripts. But why did Muslim readers and copyists have no theological objection to using the paper of the 'infidel'? The answer is that already in the fifteenth century in Northern Algeria there was a *fatwa*, or legal opinion on matters of Muslim law, that it was acceptable to use paper of Christian European origin since it was a necessity (Jeppie, 2014, p. 98).

A second feature is that Cape Muslims allowed their children to attend Christian schools where the girls stayed longer than the boys, and attained higher literacy levels.[137] At the same time, conversion of some European women to Islam through marriage stimulated the production of Islamic reading material in English and Dutch using the Roman script. One of the catechisms that Zwemer found in 1925, *The Faith of Islam and Iman*, had been written in English by *Imam* Abdurakib ibn Abdul Kahaar, and printed in Cape Town in 1914 especially for such converts. The use of the language of the 'infidel' was unusual but considered to be necessary (Davids, 2011, p. 100). This catechism was an attractive sixteen-page booklet with pictures of Mecca and Medina on the covers (Zwemer, 1925, p. 349). Similarly, in 1915, Sheikh Abdullah Ta Ha Gamieldien translated a book into Dutch to be read especially by Muslim women 'when they are idle' because 'This will be better than reading English story books and novels' (Davids, 2011, p. 101).

A third feature is that disputes between Cape Town's *Imams* made some mosques 'intense zones of conflict', and impacted the development of printing networks (Jeppie, 1996). Soliciting an Islamic view from abroad to help resolve some of these disputes underscored the value placed on access to Islamic knowledge. Those who could travel to centres of learning in Mecca and Cairo for a religious education came to be known as Sheikhs, instead of *Imams* who were locally trained. Having established their connections with global Islamic printing networks, the Sheikhs often returned from abroad with books collected from Islamic centres to teach their students. Some also returned with a basic knowledge of the printing process, and the ensuing printing business ventures was a fourth feature.

Lithographic printing became popular and more widely acceptable in the Muslim world during the nineteenth century, although the *Koran* had been printed in Arabic script as early as the fifteenth century. Lithographic printed texts were attractive to readers accustomed to using manuscripts since lithography was based directly on handwriting for the purpose of reproduction. For aesthetic reasons, characters were joined naturally instead of mechanically as in typography, and decoration was possible as

---

[137] *Imams* also taught the Bible in Muslim schools (Dick, 2012, p. 35).

in manuscripts (Messick, 2013). Its adoption provided a livelihood for some Cape Muslim scholars as writers. These distinctive reading, writing, and copying practices connected the Cape with Islamic printing networks stretching across Africa, the Western and Eastern Indian Ocean regions, as well as Asia. Scholars identify the Anjouan and Zanzibar islands, as well as the cities of Constantinople, Bombay, and Cairo, but they do not elaborate how or why these connections originated, and what their consequences were for the Cape Muslim reading community.[138]

Anjouan and Zanzibar Islands

The Cape's connections with East African and Western Indian Ocean Islamic printing networks were established much earlier than we had previously thought, and they were maintained over a long period. The Ibadi Muslim movement, which was dominant in Oman and active also in Algeria, Tunisia, and Libya, had reached East Africa already in the seventh century (Van Donzel, 1994, p. 142). Through the East Africa link, these Islamic printing networks had extended south to Cape Town by 1820 when Arab leaders from the island of Anjouan (part of the Comores today) in the Mozambique Channel started sending books to the Cape Islamic community (Rochlin, 1933). That region may well have been a source of the supply of Arabic and Malay books that were sold at the 'Foreign Book and Stationery Warehouse' – also called the 'South African Bazaar' – in the 1830s and 1840s in Cape Town

Its proprietor, Joseph Suasso De Lima, had close ties with the Cape Muslim community, and taught and employed young Muslims in his printing business. In his quest to promote reading and writing among Cape Town's common readers, De Lima's bilingual newspaper – *De Verzamelaar / The Gleaner* – carried content that appealed also to Muslim readers.[139] The Ibadis who had established the *al-Baruniyah* Lithographic

---

[138] Davids, (2011), p. 120; Haron, (2006); Tayob, (1995), pp. 68, 144–5; Van Selms, (1953), pp. 14–15.

[139] See, for example, *De Verzamelaar*, 2 July 1828; and 20 August 1839. For examples of fables and legends, see *De Verzamelaar* issues of 4 February 1826; 11 February 1826; 18 February 1826; 29 April 1826; and 6 May 1826.

Press in the nineteenth century in Cairo, also started the first Arabic printing press in Zanzibar in 1879 to produce Ibadi scholars' books (Bang, 2011; Khalīfah Nāmī, 1972, p. xviii). By the early twentieth century, some Cape Muslim scholars still stopped at Zanzibar on their return from pilgrimage in Mecca. In 1903, Sheikh Muhammad Salih, who had shipped 'hundreds of books' from Mecca to Cape Town, stopped there to collect more books for distribution, and for teaching his advanced students (Hendricks, 2005, pp. 382–4).

Constantinople

A letter from the Cape Muslim community in July 1862, channeled via Queen Victoria to Turkey's Ottoman Sultan, asked for a religious guide to be sent to settle a dispute. As a result, Abu Bakr Effendi arrived in Cape Town on 13 January 1863. Religious books relevant to this dispute that were also sent included the *Koran*, Hadith books, and catechisms by scholars such as Ghazali (Gençoğlu, 2013, p. 55). The Effendi quickly became aware of the rivalry between Christian and Muslim missionaries, and started the Ottoman Theological School in 1864 for both boys and girls; Tahora Effendi, who became his second wife at the Cape, headed the school for girls. He quickly learned and even improved the local Arabic-Afrikaans vernacular. For nearly a decade, he circulated loose pages as drafts of his *Beyan al-din* (Explanation of the religion that deals with the ritualistic practices of cleansing, prayer, religious tax, and fasting) among his students and the community, and amended it following their discussion and comments. It was printed and published in 1877 in Constantinople as the first printed book in Arabic-Afrikaans.

Beyan al-din was published as a gift from the Sultan of the Ottoman State to Muslims at the Cape of Good Hope. This gesture by an empire in decline reveals the value it placed on the role of Islamic printing networks to carry pan-Islamic ideas to the southern tip of Africa. What had remained unknown until recently was that the Effendi's *Merasid ud-din* (which deals with the slaughtering of livestock, religious prohibitions, drink, and hunting), was in fact printed together with the *Beyan al-din* as one volume to save costs during the decline of the Ottoman Empire. The *Merasid ud-din* was printed in Arabic especially for other Africans, and copies were found in Mozambique and Mauritius. The Sultan Abdul Hamid II, who had issued the decree to publish 1,500 copies of the Effendi's books in a single volume, also directed him to distribute the *Merasid ud-din* in Arabic among the people of Mozambique (Gençoğlu, 2013, pp. 95–100). In this case, the language had to meet the needs of Muslim readers in Mozambique where *Imams* and scholars probably translated it into the indigenous dialects.

Abu Bakr Effendi's nephew Omer Lufti Effendi, who came to Cape Town with his uncle in 1863, wrote a travelogue of his journey to Cape Town in Turkish that was also printed and published in 1877 in Constantinople.[140] It was subsequently translated into English for readers at the Cape. And two of Abu Bakr's son Hesham Effendi's books were published in Constantinople in 1894 and 1912, and used as handbooks at the Muslim schools where he taught in Cape Town and later in Port Elizabeth to meet the local demand for suitable school textbooks (Davids, 2011, pp. 140–3). Some of Abu Bakr Effendi's own books that he brought with him in 1863 for a school library are still extant. These publications were part of a larger oceanic movement of printed books to service a growing Islamic religious market in Southern Africa.

The reception of the *Beyan al-din*, which was shipped in bulk for distribution in Cape Town, was, however, affected by disputes among local readers (Green, 2011, p. 212). Antipathy for Abu Bakr Effendi's association with the Hanafite school of thought in a predominantly Shafite Cape Islamic community, and conflicting views about what was forbidden (*haram*), led to criticism of his *Beyan al-din*. On the other hand, it actually stimulated readers and writers to respond with their own printed products, especially after 1890. As Davids (2011, pp. 107, 137) argues, in the small and divided Cape Muslim community, writers had to be selective in their topics for publications and translations that would attract a readership.

Bombay

In 1897, following a dispute about the mispronunciation of the Arabic recitation during prayer that eventually had to be settled in court, Sheikh

---

[140] E-mail on 2 June 2014 from H. Gençoğlu.

Abdurahman ibn Muhammad al Iraki, who was originally from Basra in Iraq, wrote a book on the matter. It was printed and published in 1900 by the Nuruddin Press in Bombay, and sold very well in Cape Town (Davids, 1993, pp. 76, 81). He also produced a five-language word list with short sentences in Arabic, Farsi, Hindustani, Afrikaans, and English. This was printed and published in Bombay by Kalzar Husna Press in 1905, and was so popular that no complete copy can be found today. His choice of Bombay may be explained by its connections with his native city of Basra, which was at the heart of the *Al Nahda* printing network. In the eleventh century already there were bookshops in Basra, and 'book criers' announced the sale of manuscripts. In the *Al Nahda* period, there were guilds of booksellers, as well as copiers and binders (Ayalon, 2010, p. 76). A Christian missionary in Basra had also ordered a lithographic printing press from Bombay in July 1830 to publish a book about Basra and Iraq for an Indian audience.[141]

Cape Town's Sheikh Achmad Behardien, who was influenced by Sheikh Abdurahman ibn Muhammad al Iraki, also chose the Nuruddin Press in Bombay in 1918 to print and publish his *Su'al wa jawâb*, or, 'Questions and Answers about the Fundamental Attributes of God', in Arabic-Afrikaans. Interestingly, the last printed book in Arabic-Afrikaans in 1957, also written by Sheikh Achmad Behardien, and in which he differed from Sheikh Abdurahman ibn Muhammad al Iraki about the mid-day prayer after the Friday congregational prayer, was printed at the Mosque Shafee in Cape Town (Davids, 1993, pp. 79–80). In this instance, a local printing press had been deemed best to produce a publication on a sensitive topic in the vernacular. This confirms the printing expertise in the Cape Muslim community by that time.

Cairo

Steamship travel between Cape Town and Aden, and the building of the Suez Canal in 1869, made Cairo and Mecca accessible to more Cape Muslims (Tayob, 1995, p. 50). Besides the opportunity for pilgrimage, it was now possible for young Muslim men to study at Islamic centres in these

---

[141] A. K. Al-Rawi, *Media Practice in Iraq*, p. 7. www.palgraveconnect.com/pc/doifinder/10.1057/9781137271648.0001. Accessed 20 February 2015.

cities. A prolific writer and translator who left Cape Town in 1921 to study in Cairo and returned in 1931, was Sheikh Ismail Hanif Edwards. His most important book, a translation of a work on the practices of the people of the Hadralmaut (in Saudi Arabia), was printed and published in 1928 at a Cairo *maktaba* (bookshop). It was established in 1859 as the Mustafa al-Babi al-Halabi publisher, but had already operated as a *maktaba* since 1809. Its imprint was found especially in books in the period from 1910 to 1930, which includes the printing date for Sheikh Edwards' book, and it disseminated religious works in several African languages (Bang, 2011, p. 103).

Such *maktabas* flourished during the *Al Nahda* period and some became multi-purpose centres where paper, envelopes, notebooks, pencils, and ink were sold. They were linked to a network of printing presses, newspaper peddlers, reading clubs, educational institutions, literary societies, and journal agents. This network connected bookshops in Cairo, Beirut, Istanbul, Alexandria, Damascus, Aleppo, Tripoli, Jaffa, Tunis, and elsewhere. They advertised in their local newspapers the books sold across these cities (Ayalon, 2010, pp. 79–82, 89–90). Some *maktabas* initiated the publication of books themselves, as indicated on their title pages. Through scholars like Sheikh Edwards and other pilgrims who stopped in Cairo en route to and from Mecca, Cape Town's Muslim community forged links with these global Islamic printing networks. The Shafi tradition that was well represented in Cairo made it attractive to Cape Muslim writers, and Sheikh Edwards had several of his works printed there (Haron, 2006). He spent many hours with Cairo printers in order to proofread the Arabic-Afrikaans that was foreign to Egyptians.

He eventually used a Gestetner duplicating machine to print copies at home, after friends and students requested him to do so. His son Kaashief assisted him to produce multiple lithograph prints of his other books and translations in Arabic, Arabic-Afrikaans, English, and Afrikaans on topics requested by readers between 1928 and 1952 (Ebrahim, 2004, pp. 133–8). By the 1950s, Arabic-Afrikaans publications could no longer compete with the growing number of Islamic publications appearing in Afrikaans and English. This trend had already emerged in the early decades of the twentieth century, when Muslim readers' interests shifted towards secular and political topics. It motivated Islamic printers to produce newspapers in several languages (Mesthrie, 1997). These developments pushed local Islamic printing practices in new directions.

Cape Town

Because of its international contacts, the Cape's own Islamic printing network bore, by the 1920s, features of pan-Islamism and pan-Africanism, which worried political authorities. In October 1925, Samuel Zwemer exclaimed that:

> The Capindia Press at Cape Town also publishes four newspapers: '*The Moslem Outlook*', '*The Cape Indian*', '*The African Voice*', and '*The African World*.' The two latter are published in diglot, English and Bantu; '*The Cape Indian*' in English and Gujerati. All these weekly newspapers advocate race equality, and represent strong nationalistic tendencies.[142]

He quoted the White-owned *Cape Times* newspaper that warned that 'there is . . . a possibility that pan-Islamism may find among the Bantu a fertile field for its proselytizing seed'. Zwemer also pointed out that Islam at the Cape is coming in closer touch with Islam at the great centres in Zanzibar, Bombay, Mecca, and Cairo.

The Capindia Press (Cape Indian press) commenced printing of *The Cape Indian* newspaper in June 1922 as 'a monthly journal dealing with matters of interest to the Indian community'.[143] By August 1923, it appeared in English, Urdu, and Gujurati, and was published by the South African Indian Bureau. The Indian Muslim proprietor, Ahmed Ismail, explained that although it catered primarily for the Cape's Muslim readers, it also advertised its business of printing jobs at Hanover Street in Cape Town for all members of the community. More significantly, he announced that its aim was to advocate the cause of 'Non-Europeans in the Union'.[144] This

---

[142] *The Moslem World*, 1925, 15, pp. 330–1.

[143] *The Cape Indian*, June 1922, 1 (1), p. 1.

[144] *The Cape Indian*, October 1922, 1 (5), p. 8.

wide remit led it to carry political content of the Teachers' League of South Africa, the African Political Organization, as well as announcements of the meetings and fund-raising concerts of the African National Congress (ANC).[145]

One of its newspapers, *The Moslem Outlook* (1925–7), had a more religious outlook and enjoyed a very high circulation. It covered national and international events of interest to Muslims, and reported on the public meeting of a local 'Caliphate committee' dealing with the sudden abolition of the Caliphate by Kamal Ataturk in 1924 (Haron, 2013). But *The Moslem Outlook* also supported the more inclusive views of the African Political Organization's Dr. Abdullah Aburahman (a member of the committee) on this matter. His views, unlike those of the anti-Indian Cape Malay Association, were generally in line with *The Cape Indian* and with Ahmed Ismail's advocacy of the cause of all non-Europeans (and Muslims) in the Union of South Africa. *The Moslem Outlook* subsequently attracted the interest of James Thaele, a Cape Provincial leader of the ANC. He already had a link with *The Cape Indian* through its regular advertisement of ANC notices. Thaele founded *The African World* that appeared weekly from May 1925 to July 1926 in English, isiSotho, and isiXhosa.

Capindia Press also printed *The African Voice* or *Izwi Lama Africa*, which appeared in 1923 in English and isiXhosa (Switzer & Switzer, 1979, pp. 28–9). It had been founded in Queenstown in the Eastern Cape in 1922, by I. B. Nyombolo and Samuel Bennett Ncwana who were also ANC members. Ncwana was active in local trade union organizations and the Universal Negro Improvement Association, and he edited the short-lived newspaper *Black Man*. Not much is known about early Muslim missionary efforts to proselytize Black South Africans. Pan-Islam had, however, worried the Cape political and religious leaders more when it involved the conversion of Blacks in the 1920s than the conversion of Whites during the second half of the nineteenth century. Capindia Press raised the visibility of a growing unity among the Cape's oppressed peoples, and sought to satisfy the religious and secular demands of readers and book-buyers.

---

[145] *The Cape Indian*, October 1924, 2 (19), p. 5.

Conclusion

An obscure but important Muslim reading community connected the Cape with global Islamic printing networks. Its distinctive reading, writing, copying, and printing practices engaged the transnational Islamic book trade and stimulated the growth of local literary-cultural projects. By the early twentieth century, its pan-Islamic and pan-African printing practices prepared this reading community to challenge segregationist and, subsequently, apartheid South Africa. Its newspapers nurtured an ethos of improvement that inspired Black South Africans in the struggle against racism and inequality.

Conclusion

Readers should feature more prominently in accounts of South Africa's early literary culture. One way to achieve this is to incorporate the cultural initiatives of reading communities either overlooked, or dealt with separately and in a cursory fashion. Manfred Nathan's 1925 survey of South African literature already assumed then that it was mainly English with some Dutch, and ignored 'black or indigenous cultural production'.[146] Efforts at redress should, however, recognise that the consumption and creative literacy practices of readers are as significant as the production and creative literary outputs of writers. Dukwana, as the Introduction reveals, was not simply a reader of Tiyo Soga's translation of *The Pilgrim's Progress*. As a writer and lay preacher too, the notes in isiXhosa and English found on him may have been original commentary or critique, or thoughts and ideas for sermons. And as a translator and printer, he was possibly preparing reading material for publication in one of the vernacular newspapers.[147]

Having decided to turn against the missionaries and stand instead with his chief Sandile, Dukwana may in fact have been inspired, as Isaac Wauchope would later recommend, to 'take paper and ink' and to fire

---

[146] Noted in Dennis Walder's review of Christopher Heywood's *A History of South African Literature*. www.researchgate.net/publication/265829621_A_History_of_South_African_Literature_review. Accessed 30 January 2020.

[147] He had already helped with the production of the newspaper *Ikwezi* in 1844–5.

With his pen (Odendaal, 2012, pp. 43–4). Readers are therefore writers too, and sending letters to newspapers was a practice among Black public intellectuals and ordinary readers since the publication of the monthly *Indaba* at Lovedale in the early 1860s. It carried correspondence and columns filled by readers writing on topics that included education, justice, history, and poetry (Odendaal, 2012, p. 29; Kaschula, 2017, p. 10). Readers submitted more letters than the vernacular newspapers could manage. This developed their writing skills, and introduced them to public debate. By the 1870s, special supplements of *Isidigimi sama-Xosa* had to be printed to accommodate all the correspondents, and it was not uncommon for some issues to have more than ten letters.

In this process, Black readers and writers also acquired procedural and organisational skills. And in their own literary and mutual improvement societies many 'talks' and essays, even on reading itself, were actually read and debated. These cultural initiatives increased the number of reading spaces for literate Black South Africans who in 1921 already numbered 455,398.[148] Dukwana was the 'unnamed Xhosa soldier' for literary historian David Attwell, who appears not to have been fully aware of his background. For this reason, his 'transculturation of enlightenment into African terms' is limited by effectively excluding African readers from recasting European forms in their own terms in the long history of symbolic and political struggle in South Africa. The reading and writing practices of readers like Johann Frederick Hein, John Parkies, Jongie Siers, and Zippora Leshoai discussed in Section 1 are, however, compelling. They strengthen the case for connecting Dukwana the reader with Soga the writer in Attwell's call to rewrite modernity.

Dukwana and Soga were members of 'a class of natives who amidst much that is against them have been striving to arise and improve'.[149] As a student in Glasgow, Soga had been a member of a mutual improvement society where he was also an avid reader.[150] On Saturday mornings at Mgwali mission station back in the Eastern Cape, his own mutual

---

[148] *Report on the Third Census 1921*, 1924.

[149] Correspondence from Soga in *King William's Town Gazette*, 11 May 1865.

[150] See Bickford-Smith's (2011, p. 90) analysis of the books that Soga read.

improvement programme for young learners included reading the work of Enlightenment authors like Edward Gibbon (Chalmers, 1878, pp. 75, 166). Section 2 argued that despite their differences, reading communities in Black mutual improvement societies, English literary societies, and Dutch-Afrikaner debating societies together evinced a unique ethos of improvement in the second half of the long nineteenth century. Unifying features of this unique ethos included published books, and manuscript magazines or journals carrying members' original literary contributions; the use of editors and sub-editors, as well as members' criticism to improve the pieces for inclusion in the society's manuscript magazines and journals, as well as in newspapers; the range of languages used in society meetings, and their reportage in local newspapers; engagement with political and literary topics of the day; and their collaboration with local public libraries, which, as shared reading spaces, were freely accessible to poor Blacks and Whites.

Some of these societies' improving aims were 'rational amusement', and 'useful recreation to all classes', and where societies had a dramatic section, there were public 'entertainments' too. In these voluntary societies, Black and Dutch-Afrikaner reading communities reframed rather than rejected the 'English' rhetoric and ethos of improvement. And the translation, quotation, performance, public reading, lecturing, politicising, screening, and sermonising of Charles Dickens in Section 3 attest to his universal appeal to South African readers, critics, commentators, and theatre patrons. The public libraries, as state-subsidised voluntary societies, could satisfy Charlie Immelman's appetite for Dickens' works, and support his life-long reading career despite working in several small towns across the Cape countryside. Section 4 is also an argument that the ethos of improvement for reading communities became financially sustainable and accessible to all kinds of readers since the mid nineteenth century. More public libraries were established, and the number of daily visitors grew significantly. They would remain contested spaces, but became permanent fixtures on the South African reading landscape.

As in the history of the book in Africa, Eurocentric models and ideas cannot fully explain the complexities and multiplicity of contexts in the history of reading in Africa (Davis & Johnson, 2015). In a recent overview of fundamental questions and propositions in the history of reading, with a view to suggesting approaches to analyse 'reading practices in modern times', there is still no mention of Africa or Asia (Chartier, 2017). A predominantly Judeo-Christian and Northern European frame of reference cannot therefore adequately explain why and how a small Muslim community at the Cape connected with global Islamic printing networks. Section 5 shows how the production of pan-Islamic and pan-African books and newspapers, inspired by the *Nahda* or Arab project of Enlightenment, nurtured an ethos of improvement among Cape Muslims. Enlightenment ideas about natural rights and the wider struggle against racism and inequality had already featured in the reading of indigenous South Africans in the early nineteenth century (Dick, 2018, pp. 398–400).

The history of the book and of reading in Africa therefore asks 'quite different questions', and applies quite different propositions and approaches from those familiar in Northern Europe (Johnson & Davis, 2015, p. 5). In South Africa, a religiously infused ethos of improvement dominant in the eighteenth and early nineteenth centuries gradually transformed into a more politically and culturally infused ethos of improvement. Disillusionment in the second half of the nineteenth century invested 'the literary' and the encouragement to read and to debate with a stronger political purpose (Odendaal, 2012, p. 57). As a consequence, literature as a moralising force to 'improve' readers also acquired a stronger sense of its political commitments (Hofmeyr, 2006, p. 269). Striving to secure their interests in a search for independence and self-empowerment, reading communities in English, Dutch-Afrikaner, and Black voluntary societies nurtured a unique South African ethos of improvement.

How this happened is now clearer as the result of the evidence produced in this Element. Future research will benefit from further analysis, and revisiting David Attwell's seminal ideas. It will reveal more about South Africa's unique politically and culturally infused ethos of improvement in twentieth century voluntary societies. It will also explain whether or not 'transculturated enlightenment', as Attwell speculated, indeed resurfaced in the early 1990s as 'the recovery of human rights'.

Appendix

Sample of South African reading spaces, ca. 1850–1920

Town	Founded	First printing	First public/ subscription library established	Voluntary associations	Early and contemporary newspapers
Aliwal North	1849	1870	1870	Reading Association/ Mutual Improvement Society (1874)/ Literary entertainment (1870s)	*Aliwal Observer/Aliwal North Standard*
Bloemfontein	1846	1850	1867 (traveling library)	Literary, Scientific, and Debating Societies (1870s)	*Friend of the Sovereignty/ Bloemfontein Gazette/ De Tijd*
Cape Town	1652	1784	1818 (South African Public Library)	Mutual Improvement Societies (1874)/ Mechanics Institutes (1870s)/ Literary & Debating Societies	*Cape Argus/Cape Town Daily News/Standard and Mail/Cape Times*
Cradock	1813	1850	1865	Reading Society (1840s)/ Literary entertainment (1870s)	*Cradock & Tarkastad Register/Cradock Express*

Cont.

Town	Founded	First printing	First public/ subscription library established	Voluntary associations	Early and contemporary newspapers
Dordrecht	1856	1872	1890	Wodehouse Literary Society (1870s)	*Aliwal Observer and Dordrecht and Lady Grey Times*
Durban	1835	1850/1	1853	Mechanics Institute (1853)	*D'Urban Observer/Natal Times/Natal Mercury*
Graaff-Reinet	1786	1851	1847	Reading Society proposed (June 1853) Literary Society (early 1900s)	*Graaff-Reinet Courant/ Graaff-Reinet Herald*
Graham's Town	1812	1831	1841	Reading Society (1830)/ Mutual Improvement Society (1860s)	*Grahamstown Journal/ Great Eastern/Eastern Star*
Kimberley	1871	1870	1882	Literary & Debating Society/ Mutual Improvement Society (1890s)	*Diamond Field/Diamond Fields Advertiser*

Lovedale	1824	1861	1868	Literary Society (1879)	Indaba/Isigidimi SamaXhosa/Imvo Zabantsundu
Pietermaritzburg	1838	1844	1849 (Natal Society Library)	Book/Reading Society (1846)/ Natal Literary Society (1851)	De Natalier & Pietermaritzburg True Recorder/Natal Witness
Port Elizabeth	1820	1845	1848	Book Society (1830s)/ Mechanics Institute (late 19th century)	Eastern Province Herald/ Port Elizabeth Mercury
Pretoria	1855	1857	1878	Literary and Debating Society	Staats Courant der ZAR
Queenstown	1853	1859	1859	Mutual Improvement Society (1860s)	Queenstown Free Press
Robertson	1853	No date given	1872	Mutual Improvement Society (1883)/ Literary Society (1905)	Oudtshoorn Courant/ Worcester Courant (nearby towns)
Stellenbosch	1679	1859	1859	Reading Club (1849)	De Zuid-Afrikaan/ Lees-Vruchten

Cont.

Town	Founded	First printing	First public/ subscription library established	Voluntary associations	Early and contemporary newspapers
Swellendam	1745	1859	1838	Book/Reading society (1834/1852)/ Literary Institute (1857)/ Play Reading Society (1903)	*Overberg Courant*
Uitenhage	1804	1864	1858	Reading Society (1825)/ Literary and Debating Society (1886)	*The Uitenhage Times*
Worcester	1820	1865	1854	Literary Society (1860s)	*Worcester Courant*
Other towns with Reading/ Literary/ Debating Societies since the 1850s	Barkly West, Claremont, Graaff-Reinet, Greytown, Isipingo, Middelburg, Newcastle, Richmond (Cape and Natal colonies), Stanger, Verulam.				

Some towns with Dutch-Afrikaans Debating Societies since the 1870s	Komga-Diepkloof, Vlekpoort, Bruintjieshoogte, Biesiesvlei, Oudtshoorn, Stellenbosch, Stanford Klein Drakenstein, Magaliesberg, Boven Vallei, Hartebeestrivier, and many others.
Some towns with African Mutual Improvement Societies since the 1880s	Burnshill; D'Urban; Healdtown; Butterworth (Gcuwa and Transkei Mutual Improvement Association); Peddie (D'Urban Teachers' Mutual Improvement Association); Port Elizabeth; Thaba 'Nchu (Becoana Mutual Improvement Society); Kimberley (South Africans Improvement Society).

References

Aliwal North Public Library Catalogue of Books. (1903). Aliwal North: Northern Post.

Attwell, D. (2006). *Rewriting Modernity: Studies in Black South African Literary History*. Athens: Ohio University Press.

Ayalon, A. (2008). Private Publishing in the Nahda. *International Journal of Middle Eastern Studies*, 40, 561–77.

Ayalon, A. (2010). Arab Booksellers and Bookshops in the Age of Printing, 1850–1914. *British Journal of Middle Eastern Studies*, 37, 73–93.

Baker, J. (1862). Literary Reminiscences. In *Literary Recreations: A Selection of Lectures*, Swellendam: Pike & Byles, pp. 91–109.

Bang, A. (2011). Authority and Piety, Writing and Print: A Preliminary Study of the Circulation of Islamic Texts in Late Nineteenth- and Early Twentieth-Century Zanzibar. *Africa: The Journal of the International African Institute*, 81, 89–107.

Barkly West Public Library and Reading Room Catalogue of Books. Grahamstown: Grocott & Sherry.

Bassett, T. J. (2017). Evidence of Reading: The Social Network of the Heath Book Club. *Victorian Studies*, 59 (3), 426–35.

Bickford-Smith, V. (1995). Black Ethnicities, Communities and Political Expression in Late Victorian Cape Town. *Journal of African History*, 36, 443–65.

Bickford-Smith, V. (2003). Words, Wars and World Views: The Coming of Literacy and Books to Southern Africa. *Bulletin du Bibliophile*, 1, 9–22.

Bickford-Smith, V. (2011). African Nationalist or British Loyalist? The Complicated Case of Tiyo Soga. *History Workshop Journal*, 71 (1), 74–97.

Biewenga, A. (1996). Alfabetisering Aan de Kaap de Goede Hoop Omstreeks 1700. *Tydskrif vir Nederlands en Afrikaans*, 3 (2), 109–21.

Boer, N. (2017) Exploring British India: South African Prisoners of War as Imperial Travel Writers, 1899–1902. *Journal of Commonwealth Literature*, 54 (3), 429–43. (2019).

Booyens, B. (1983). '*Ek heb geseg*': *Die Verhaal van ons Jongeliede- en Debatsverenigings*. Kaapstad: Human & Rousseau.

Bosman, F. C. L. (1980). *Drama en Toneel in Suid-Afrika, Deel II, 1856–1912*. Pretoria: Van Schaik.

Brake, L. (2017). The Serial and the Book in Nineteenth-Century Britain: Intersections, Extensions, Transformations. *Mémoires du livre*, 8 (2), 1–16.

Brink, J. N. (1960). Kultuurbrokkies uit die Krygsgevangekamp, Diyatalawa. *Historia*, 5 (4), 261–66.

Broadbent, S. (1865). *A Narrative of the First Introduction of Christianity amongst the Baralong Tribe of Bechuanas, South Africa*. London: Wesleyan Mission House.

Cape of Good Hope Blue Books, 1858–1909. Cape Town: Solomon.

Cape Town Police Library. (1846). Cape Town: De Lima.

Census of the Colony of the Cape of Good Hope, 1865. (1866). Cape Town: Saul Solomon.

Chalmers, J. A. (1878). *Tiyo Soga: A Page of South African Mission Work*. Edinburgh: Andrew Elliot.

Chartier, R. (2017). From Texts to Readers: Literary Criticism, Sociology of Practice and Cultural History. *Estudios Históricos Rio de Janerio*, 30 (62), 741–56.

Child, D. (1979). *A Merchant Family in Early Natal: Diaries and Letters of Joseph and Marianne Churchill, 1850–1880*. Cape Town: Balkema.

Christison, G. (2012). Readers and Writers in Colonial Natal (1843–1910). *English in Africa*, 39 (2), 111–33.

Clark, A. (1897). *Paper on Art and the New Woman: Read before the Ladies' Pioneer Debating Club and Art Section of the Riebeeck College Guild*. Uitenhage: Sellick.

Conradie, E. J. (1934). *Hollandse Skrywers uit Suid-Afrika: 'n Kultuur-Historische Studie. Deel 1 (1652–1875)*. Pretoria: De Bussy.

Conradie, W. S. (1985). *Goue Jubileum NG Kerk Biesiesvlei, 1935–1985*. No place and publisher.

Cook, P. A. W. (1939). *The Native Std.VI Pupil: A Socio-Educational Survey of Std. VI Pupils in Native Schools in the Union of South Africa, 1935*. Pretoria: South African Council for Educational and Social Research.

Cope, J. (1950). Charles Dickens, the Radical. *Guardian*, 20 July, 4.

Couzens, T. (1984). Widening Horizons of African Literature, 1870–1900. In L. White & T. Couzens, eds., *Literature and Society in South Africa*. Cape Town: Maskew Miller, pp. 60–80.

Darnton, R. (1982). What is the History of Books? *Daedalus*, 111, 65–83.

Davenport, T. R. H. (1973). The History of Race Relations in South Africa. *Zambezia*, 3 (1): 5–14.

Davids, A. (1990). Words the Cape Slaves Made: A Socio-historical-linguistic Study, *South African Journal of Linguistics*, 8 (1), 1–24.

Davids, A. (1993). The Early Afrikaans Publications and Manuscripts in Arabic Script. In P. E. Westra & B. Warner, eds., *Festschrift in Honour of Frank R. Bradlow*. Cape Town: Friends of the South African Library, pp. 67–82.

Davids, A. (2011). *The Afrikaans of the Cape Muslims from 1815 to 1915*, H. Willemse & S. E. Dangor, eds., Pretoria: Protea Book House.

Davis, C., & Johnson, D., eds. (2015). *The Book in Africa: Critical Debates*. Basingstoke, Hampshire: Palgrave Macmillan.

Davis, J. R. (2018). *Tiyo Soga: A Literary History*. Unisa Press.

Delmas, A. (2014). *Artem Quaevis Terra Alit*: Books in the Cape Colony During the Seventeenth and Eighteenth Centuries. In N. M. Alvarez, ed., *Books in the Catholic World in the Early Modern Period*. Leiden: Koninklijke Brill, pp. 191–214.

Dick, A. L. (2012). *The Hidden History of South Africa's Book and Reading Cultures*. Toronto: University of Toronto Press.

Dick, A. L. (2015). Copying and Circulation in South Africa's Reading Cultures, 1780–1840. In C. Davis & D. Johnson, eds., *The Book in Africa: Critical Debates*, Basingstoke, Hampshire: Palgrave Macmillan, pp. 21–43.

Dick, A. L. (2018). Reading Authors of the Enlightenment at the Cape of Good Hope from the late 1780s to the mid-1830s, *Journal of Southern African Studies*, 44 (3), 383–400.

Drennan, M. R. (1900). *Gogga Brown: The Life-Story of Alfred Brown, South Africa's Hermit-Naturalist: Told from his Journal*. Cape Town: Miller.

Dubow, S. (2006). *A Commonwealth of Knowledge: Science, Sensibility, and White South Africa, 1820–2000*. Oxford: Oxford University Press.

Duff, S. E. (2011). 'Onschuldig Vermaak': The Dutch Reformed Church and Children's Leisure Time in the Nineteenth-Century Cape Colony, *South African Historical Journal*, 63 (4), 495–513.

Ebrahim, M. H. (2004). *Shaykh Ismail Hanif Edwards*. Cape Town.

Elbourne, E., & Ross, R. (1997). Combating Spiritual and Social Bondage: Early Missions in the Cape Colony. In R. Elphick & R. Davenport, eds., *Christianity in South Africa: A Political, Cultural, and Social History*. Oxford: Currey, pp. 31–50.

Faure, D. P. (1907). *My Life and Times*. Cape Town: Juta.

Fletcher, J. (1994). *The Story of Theatre in South Africa: A Guide to its History from 1780–1930*. Cape Town: Vlaeberg.

Forrest, J. (1907). South Africa's Favourite Novelists. *The African Monthly*, 1, 69–73.

Fourie, J., Ross, R., & Viljoen, R. (2013). *Literacy at South African Mission Stations*. Stellenbosch University: Bureau for Economic Research.

Gençoğlu, H. (2013). Abu Bakr Effendi: A Report on the Activities and Challenges of an Ottoman Muslim Theologian in the Cape of Good Hope. University of Cape Town. Masters dissertation.

Giliomee, H. (1991). The Beginnings of Afrikaner Ethnic Consciousness, 1850–1915. In L. Vail, ed., *The Creation of Tribalism in Southern Africa*. Berkeley: University of California Press, pp. 21–54.

Glynn, T. (2018). Reading Publics: Books, Communities and Readers in the Early History of American Public Libraries. In K. Roberts & M. Towsey, eds., *Before the Public Library: Reading, Community, and Identity in the Atlantic World, 1650–1850*. Leiden: Brill, pp. 323–48.

Green, N. (2011). *Bombay Islam: The Religious Economy of the West Indian Ocean, 1840–1915*. New York: Cambridge University Press.

Gutsche, T. (1972). *History and Social Significance of Motion Pictures in South Africa, 1895–1940*. Cape Town: Timmins.

Haron, M. (2006). The Production of the South African 'Muslim Book': A Means of Empowerment and a Source of Identity. In C. Ovens, ed., *Bibliophilia Africana 8: From Papyrus to Print-Out; The Book in Africa*. Cape Town: National Library of South Africa, pp. 18–47.

Haron, M. (2013). The Experience of the Muslims in South Africa. Online. www.academia.edu/4111541/South_Africa_Muslims_Draft_Springer_Text_2013. Accessed 15 January 2015.

Harris, M. H. (1971). *Reader in American Library History*. Washington, DC: NCR Microcard.

Harris, M. G. (1977). *British Policy Towards the Malays at the Cape of Good Hope*, 1795–1850. Western Washington State College. Masters dissertation.

Hattersley, A. (1951). *A Victorian Lady at the Cape*. Cape Town: Miller.

Hattersley, A. (1973). *An Illustrated Social History of South Africa*. Cape Town: Balkema.

Hendricks, S. (2005). *Tasawwuf (Sufism): Its Role and Impact on the Culture of Cape Islam*. Pretoria: University of South Africa. Masters dissertation.

Hodgson, J. (1986). Soga and Dukwana: The Christian Struggle for Liberation in Mid-19th Century South Africa. *Journal of Religion in Africa*, 16 (3), 187–208.

Hofmeyr, I. (2006). Reading Debating/Debating Reading: The Case of the Lovedale Literary Society, Or Why Mandela Quotes Shakespeare. In K. Barber, ed., *Africa's Hidden Histories: Everyday Literacy and Making of the Self*. Indiana: Indiana University Press, pp. 258–277.

Hofmeyr, J. H., & Reitz, F.W. (1913). *The Life of Jan Hendrik Hofmeyr*. Cape Town: Van der Sandt.

Humpherys, A. (2011). Victorian Stage Adaptations and Novel Appropriations. In S. Ledger & H. Furneaux, eds., *Charles Dickens in Context*. Cambridge: Cambridge University Press, pp. 27–34.

Immelman, R. F. M. (1956). A Mechanics Institute in Cape Town (1853–1878). *Quarterly Bulletin of the South African Library*, 11, 17–27.

Immelman, R. F. M. (1970). Subscription Libraries in Historical Perspective: Their Use and Some Users, 1828–1950. *South African Libraries*, 38 (2), 74–85.

Jappie, S. (2012). Jawi Dari Jauh: 'Malays' in South Africa through Text. *Indonesia and the Malay World*, 40, 143–59.

Jeppie, S. (1996). Leadership and Loyalties: The Imams of Nineteenth Century Colonial Cape Town, South Africa. *Journal of Religion in Africa*, 26, 139–62.

Jeppie, S. (2014). Writing, Books, and Africa, *History and Theory*, 53, 94–104.

Johnson, D. & Davis, C. (2015). Introduction. In D. Johnson & C. Davis, eds., *The Book in Africa: Critical Debates*. Basingstoke, Hampshire: Palgrave Macmillan, pp. 1–17.

Jones, W. (1850). *The Jubilee Memorial of the Religious Tract Society, Containing a Record of its Origin, Proceedings and Results, AD 1799–1849*. London: Religious Tract Society.

Kaarsholm, P. (2014). Zanzibaris or Amakhuwa? Sufi networks in South Africa, Mozambique and the Indian Ocean, *Journal of African History*, 55, 191–210.

Kaschula, R. H. (2017). Intellectualisation of isiXhosa literature: The Case of Jeff Opland. *Tydskrif vir Letterkunde*, 54 (2), 5–25.

Kasrils, R. (1998). *Armed and Dangerous: From Undercover Struggle to Freedom*. Johannesburg: Jonathan Ball.

Khalīfah Nāmī, A. (1972). *Studies in Ibāḍism (al-Ibāḍīyah)*. Benghazi: University of Libya.

Langenhoven, C. J. (1914). *Ons Weg Deur die Wereld, en Andere Stukkies en Brokkies Oue en Nieuwe*. Potchefstroom: Het Westen Drukkerij.

Lewis, P. (1987). *The Story of a Drummer Boy and His Family: A Lewis Family History*. Johannesburg: Homstead Litho.

Ludlow, H. (2012). The Government Teacher as Mediator of a Superior Education in Colesberg, 1849–1858. *Historia*, 57 (1), 141–64.

Mansfield, P. G. (2000). *Public Libraries in Ballaratt, 1851–1900*. Deakin University. PhD thesis.

Marais, J. L. (2009). Die Invloed van die Boland op die Werk van Eugene N. Marais. *Suid-Afrikaanse Tydskrif vir Kultuurgeskiedenis*, 23 (1), 74–89.

Masilela, N. (2010). African Intellectual and Literary Responses to Colonial Modernity in South Africa. In P. Limb, N. Etherington, & P. Midgley, eds., *Grappling with the Beast: Indigenous Southern African Responses to Colonialism, 1840–1930*. Leiden: Brill, pp. 245–75.

Martin, S. K. (2014). Tracking Reading in Nineteenth-Century Melbourne Diaries. *Australian Humanities Review*, 56, 27–54.

Messick, B. (2013). On the Question of Lithography. In G. Roper, ed., *The History of the Book in the Middle East*. Farnham: Ashgate, pp. 299–317.

Mesthrie, U.S. (1997). From Advocacy to Mobilisation: *Indian Opinion*, 1903–1914. In L. Switzer, ed., *South Africa's Alternative Press: Voices of Protest and Resistance, 1880–1960*. Cambridge, Cambridge University Press, pp. 99–126.

Middleton, J. (1998). *Convictions: A Woman Political Prisoner Remembers*. Randburg: Ravan Press.

Mountain, A. (2004). *An Unsung Heritage: Perspectives on Slavery*. Claremont: David Philip.

Murray, R. M. (1894). *South African Reminiscences*. Cape Town: Juta.

Nathan, M. (1925). *South African Literature: A General Survey*. Cape Town: Juta.

Na Vyftig Jaar: Gedenkboek van die Unie-Debatsvereniging, Stellenbosch. (1926). Stellenbosch: Pro Ecclesia Drukkery.

Nienaber, P. J. (1947). *Die Vrystaatse Taalbeweging, (1900 tot ongeveer 1920)*. Johannesburg: Afrikaanse Pers-Boekhandel.

Odendaal, A. (1984). *Black Protest Politics in South Africa to 1912*. Totowa: Barnes & Noble.

Odendaal, A. (1993). Even White Boys Call Us 'Boy'! Early Black Organisational Politics in Port Elizabeth. *Kronos*, 20, 3–16.

Odendaal, A. (2012). *The Founders: The Origins of the ANC and the Struggle for Democracy in South Africa*. Johannesburg: Jacana.

Opland, J. (2003). Fighting with the Pen: The Appropriation of the Press by Early Xhosa Writers. In J. A. Draper, ed., *Orality, Literacy and Colonialism in Southern Africa*. Atlanta: Society of Biblical Literature, pp. 9–40.

Opland, J. (2004). Nineteenth-century Xhosa literature. *Kronos*, 30, 24–46.

Paleker, G. (2014). The State, Citizens, and Control: Film and African Audiences in South Africa, 1910–1948. *Journal of Southern African Studies*, 40 (2), 309–22.

Paterson, D. A., & Bryant, I. E. (1906). *Railway Institute of Salt River Library Catalogue*. Cape Town: Cape Times.

Peters, M. A. (1974). The Contribution of the (Carnegie) Non-European Library Service, Transvaal, to the Development of Library Services for Africans in South Africa: An Historical and Evaluative Study. University of Cape Town. Masters dissertation.

Peterson, B. (1989). Khabi Mngoma: Criss-Crossing Cultural Lines with the Syndicate of African Artists: A Conversation With Bhekizizwe Peterson. In Peter N. Thuynsma, ed., *Footprints Along The Way: A Tribute to Es'kia Mphahlele*. Braamfontein: Skotaville, pp. 28–34.

Plaatje, S. (1916). *Sechuana Proverbs with Literal Translations and their European Equivalents*. London: Kegan Paul.

Plug, C. (1993). Mechanics' Institutes in 19th century South Africa. *South African Journal of Higher Education*, 7 (3), 97–101.

Prinsloo, P. J. J. (1995). Die Pietermaritzburg se Debat en Letterkundige Vereniging, 1908–1918. *Historia*, 40 (1), 72–89.

Prinsloo, M., & Baynham, M. (2008). Renewing Literacy Studies. In M. Prinsloo & M. Baynham, eds., *Literacies, Global and Local*. Amsterdam: John Benjamins, pp. 1–13.

Proceedings at the Twenty Eighth Anniversary Meeting of the Subscribers to the Public Library. (1857). Cape Town: Saul Solomon.

Public Library Cape of Good Hope. (1844). *Annual Report and Supplementary Catalogue*. Cape Town: Saul Solomon.

Rainier, M., ed. (1974). *The Journals of Sophia Pigot, 1819–1821*. Cape Town: Balkema.

Read, J. (1852). *The Kat River Settlement in 1851: Described in a Series of Letters Published in the South African Commercial Advertiser.* Cape Town: Saul Solomon.

Report on the Third Census of the Union of South Africa, 1921. (1924). Pretoria: Government Printer.

Results of a Census of the Colony of the Cape of Good Hope on the Night of Sunday the 5th April 1891. (1892). Cape Town: Richards.

Rhoda, E. (2007). 'The Islamic *Da'wah* From the Auwal Masjid in the Bo-Kaap to Mosterd Bay (Strand), 1792–1838.' *Quarterly Bulletin of the National Library of South Africa*, 61, 45–56.

Rochlin, S. A. (1933). Early Arabic Printing at the Cape of Good Hope. *Bulletin of the School of Oriental Studies*, 7, 49–54.

Rochlin, S. A. (1957). Charles Dickens and the Nineteenth Century Cape. *Quarterly Bulletin of the South African Library*, 11, 87–96.

Rothmann, M. E. (1947). 'n Ou Biblioteek. *Suid-Afrikaanse Biblioteke*, 15 (2), 65–8.

Rules and Regulations of the Cape Town Literary and Debating Society. Cape Town: Saul Solomon, 1845.

Rutherfoord, E., & Murray, J. (1968). *In Mid-Victorian Cape Town: Letters from Miss Rutherfoord.* Cape Town: Balkema.

Saunders, C. (2010). Reactions to Colonialism in Southern Africa: Some Historiographical Reflections. In P. Limb, N. Etherington, and P. Midgley, eds., *Grappling with the Beast: Indigenous Southern African Responses to Colonialism, 1840–1930.* Leiden: Brill, pp. 11–19.

Schaafsma, A. (2005). Carel Pieter Immelman and his diaries, 1885–1928. *Philobiblion, Journal of the Society of Bibliophiles in Cape Town*, 3 (20), 1–10.

Shell, R. C-H. (2000). Islam in Southern Africa, 1652–1998. In N. Levistzion and R. L. Pouwels, eds., *The History of Islam in Africa.* Athens: Ohio University Press, pp. 327–48.

Shell, R. (2006). *Madrasahs* and Moravians: Muslim Educational Institutions in the Cape Colony, 1792 to 1910. *New Contree*, 51, 101–13.

Strassberger, E. (1969). *The Rhenish Mission Society in South Africa, 1830–1950.* Cape Town: Struik.

Switzer, L. (1997). The Beginnings of African Protest Journalism at the Cape. In L. Switzer, ed., *South Africa's Alternative Press: Voices of Protest and Resistance, 1880–1960.* Cambridge: Cambridge University Press, pp. 57–82.

Switzer, L, & Switzer, D. (1979). *The Black Press in South Africa and Lesotho: A Descriptive Bibliographic Guide to African, Coloured and Indian Newspapers, Newsletters and Magazines, 1836–1976.* Boston, MA: G.K. Hall.

Tayob, A. (1995). *Islamic Resurgence in South Africa: The Muslim Youth Movement.* Cape Town: UCT Press.

Traue, J. E. (2016). Eighty Years of Serial Fiction in New Zealand Newspapers: A Snapshot of Writers and their Readers. *Script & Print*, 40 (3), 144–53.

Tyamzashe, G. (1884). A Native Society at Kimberley. *The Christian Express*, 1 April 1884.

Van der Bank, D. A. (1993). Jongeliede- en Debatsverenigings in die Oranjerivierkolonie. *Researches of the National Museum*, 9 (13), 418–30.

Van der Spuy, S. J. (1913). *Jong Zuid-Afrika voor Debatverenigingen, Chr. Jongelieden Verenigingen en Dingansdag.* Paarl, Paarl Drukpers.

Van der Walt, M.S. (1972). Staatsteun aan Subskripsiebiblioteke in die Kaapkolonie vanaf 1818 tot 1919. University of Stellenbosch. Masters Dissertation.

Van Selms, A. (1953). Die Afrikaanse Literatuur van die Moslem Gemeenskap, *Suid Afrika*, 12, 14–15.

Van Donzel, E. J., ed. (1994). *Islamic Desk Reference: Compiled from the Encyclopedia of Islam.* Leiden: Brill.

Varley, D. (1958). *South African Reading in Earlier Days.* Johannesburg: SABC.

Volz, S. (2007). Words of Batswana: Letters to the Editor of 'Mahoko a Becoana', 1883–1896. *History in Africa*, 34, 349–66.

Voss, M. (2012). *Urbanizing the North-Eastern Frontier: The Frontier Intelligentsia and the Making of Colonial Queenstown, c.1859–1877.* University of Cape Town. Masters dissertation.

Weiss, L. J. (2017). The Literary Clubs and Societies of Glasgow in the Long Nineteenth Century: A City's History of Reading through its Communal Reading Practices and Productions. University of Sterling. PhD thesis.

Whiteside, J. (1906). *History of the Wesleyan Methodist Church of South Africa.* London: Elliot Stock.

Willan, B. (1984). *Sol Plaatjie: A Biography.* Johannesburg: Ravan.

Willemse, H., and Dangor, S. E., eds. (2011). *Achmat Davids: The Afrikaans of the Cape Muslims from 1815 to 1915.* Pretoria: Protea Book House.

Words of Batswana: Letters to Mahoko a Becwana, 1883–1986. (2006). Translated and edited by P. T. Magadla and S. C. Volz. Cape Town: Van Riebeeck Society.

Wright, L. (2008). Cultivating Grahamstown: Nathaniel Merriman, Shakespeare and Books. *Shakespeare in Southern Africa*, 20, 25–37.

Zwemer, S. (1925). Editorial: Islam at Cape Town, *The Moslem World*, 15, 330–1; Two Moslem Catechisms (Published at Cape Town), *The Moslem World*, 15, 349.

Cambridge Elements ☰

Publishing and Book Culture

SERIES EDITOR
Samantha Rayner
University College London

Samantha Rayner is a Reader in UCL's Department of
Information Studies. She is also Director of UCL's Centre for
Publishing, co-Director of the Bloomsbury CHAPTER
(Communication History, Authorship, Publishing, Textual
Editing and Reading) and co-editor of the Academic Book of the
Future BOOC (Book as Open Online Content) with UCL Press.

ASSOCIATE EDITOR
Leah Tether
University of Bristol

Leah Tether is Professor of Medieval Literature and Publishing
at the University of Bristol. With an academic background in
medieval French and English literature and a professional
background in trade publishing, Leah has combined her
expertise and developed an international research profile in
book and publishing history from manuscript to digital.

ADVISORY BOARD

Simone Murray, Monash University

Claire Squires, University of Stirling

Andrew Nash, University of London

Leslie Howsam, Ryerson University

David Finkelstein, University of Edinburgh

Alexis Weedon, University of Bedfordshire

Alan Staton, Booksellers Association

Angus Phillips, Oxford International Centre for Publishing

Richard Fisher, Yale University Press

John Maxwell, Simon Fraser University

Shafquat Towheed, The Open University

Jen McCall, Emerald Publishing

ABOUT THE SERIES

This series aims to fill the demand for easily accessible, quality texts available for teaching and research in the diverse and dynamic fields of Publishing and Book Culture. Rigorously researched and peer-reviewed Elements will be published under themes, or 'Gatherings'. These Elements should be the first check point for researchers or students working on that area of publishing and book trade history and practice: we hope that, situated so logically at Cambridge University Press, where academic publishing in the UK began, it will develop to create an unrivalled space where these histories and practices can be investigated and preserved.

Cambridge Elements ☰

Publishing and Book Culture

Academic Publishing
Gathering Editor: Jane Winters
Jane Winters is Professor of Digital Humanities at the School
of Advanced Study, University of London. She is co-convenor
of the Royal Historical Society's open-access monographs
series, New Historical Perspectives, and a member of the
International Editorial Board of Internet Histories and the
Academic Advisory Board of the Open Library of Humanities.

ELEMENTS IN THE GATHERING

A full series listing is available at: www.cambridge.org/EPBC

Printed in the United States
By Bookmasters